Healthy
Relationships

How to Deal with Jealousy and Attachment in Love, Overcome Conflict and Anxiety, Insecurity & Negative Thinking and improve the Couple Communication.

SARA WHITE

Contents

Introduction

Couples' therapy for healthy relationships is meant to help you understand not just yourself, but your partner as well. How to have, build up to, and maintain a healthy relationship often eludes us all. Could this be because we expect our partner to think like us? Could this be because we are conditioned to believe that true love is not just an emotion, but finding "the one" for us? Romanticizing a relationship is a choice that couples make. However, relationships are not built on romance and seduction alone. In this book, you will find the tools you need to answer all of your questions about a long-term relationship.

The question is often asked, "how do I find my soulmate?" The word soulmate itself suggests that we, as people, do not have a choice as to whom our life partner will be. The unfortunate truth here is that some people who are already in long-term relationships will ask themselves, "is this my soulmate?" The age-old quest for perfection in love and commitment appears to be a top priority. The idea of perfection in a relationship has been romanticized by the media and books. The simple and yet very delicate truth is that perfection is not the answer. Healthy long-term relationships develop through communication. As people, we hear ourselves talking, but are we truly listening?

It is common behavior for a person to believe that another person would behave, act, and respond the same way as themselves. This is so common that it is a leading cause of conflict in a relationship. How a couple communicates with one another takes time, patience, and the realization that no two people are alike. When two people find common ground, the relationship begins with a foundation of their similarities. Their similarities are often attraction, likes, dislikes, hobbies, and shared interests. An important factor in these similarities is understanding what makes them similarities. An example here would be two people that both enjoy race car driving. That alone is a great foundation to start with. The discussion, however, should include which part of racing each person likes. One person may enjoy race cars and how they drive. The other may be more interested in the drivers themselves, and what draws them into driving. Without these points being clear, the possibility of conflict is already unintentionally brewing.

During the communication process, one of the key factors is to understand how each of the partners responds to action and reaction. A couple that has been together for a year or longer will have an idea as to how to approach each other with questions or concerns. The question is the action, and the answer is the reaction. The idea is to learn how to approach your partner using a positive action and how to receive a positive reaction in return. An example here would be addressing healthy eating habits. One partner suggests to the other that they may need to start eating healthier for the greater good of their health. A healthy discussion should be direct and open to feedback.

Partner 1 — I was thinking about how we eat and our health. I think we should consider not dining at fast food places anymore, so that we can take care of our bodies.

Partner 2 — Well, I agree with eating healthier. However, with my work schedule fast food is the cheapest and easiest way for me to get my meals.

Partner 1 — We could work out our time management so that we can implement a healthier diet for us both.

Partner 2 — Okay, we could start on that and see what we come up with.

The previous example is positive communication with action and reaction. The same conversation has the potential to go in the opposite direction when words, tone, and intentions are taken the wrong way. Partner 1's first comment suggested that changing eating habits should be done together and eating healthier would assist with staying healthy. Partner 2 was already on the defense because of her work schedule. However, her reaction was still positive because she was accepting the suggestion. Had partner 1 used language that sounded like only partner 2 needed to change her eating habits, an argument would likely ensue. This couple has already begun the couples' therapy for a healthy relationship by including both partners in a healthy living lifestyle.

In the next chapter, we'll discuss the initial attraction between two people that have the potential of building a relationship. Understanding the initial attraction is crucial for couples, as well. Oftentimes, once a couple has been together for a long period of time, the very basics of attraction are forgotten. For couples' therapy, whether it's a brand-new relationship or one that has been going on for years, going back to step one shows couples how to deal with attraction.

ONE

Understanding the Initial Attraction

THERE ARE many variables in the initial attraction between two people. It is never the same for everyone because of the many variables and possibilities of meeting another individual that could be a partner. Here are some of the variables that determine initial attraction:

1. Appearance is in most cases the first thing that one would notice in a potential partner.
2. How approachable someone is.
3. The way an individual speaks to other people.
4. The personality and behavior of an individual.
5. Sexuality and communication through body language.

The very reason for so many variables is because no two people are alike. Attraction that would be a positive factor for one person could very well be a negative factor for another. To have a better understanding as to why this happens, we'll explain each variable in greater detail.

. . .

1. Appearance is in most cases the first thing that one would notice for a potential partner.

In general, an individual has an idea of how they like to dress, or how much work to put into personal appearance. Someone that spends a great deal of time ironing their clothes would find this attractive in another person. The same happens for people who find comfort in dressing in a casual manner. People in general look for a potential partner that has a similar appearance as themselves. At the very least, has an idea of how to dress for the occasion.

2. How approachable someone is.

It is often difficult to speak to someone who appears to not want to be bothered. This is because of the fear of rejection. A welcoming smile creates a lighter atmosphere for the approach. It can be just as difficult to approach a potential partner when they appear to be very outgoing. An outgoing personality is very approachable, but also easily distracted. The approach is based on the personalities of both parties. Although initial attraction is just the beginning of a relationship, it is an important part of a healthy relationship early on. Welcoming or opening conversations already determines how a couple will communicate later in the relationship.

3. The way an individual speaks to other people.

The opening conversation can be like a pop quiz that you didn't study for. The attraction continues here when there is common ground in how you speak with the other person. The use of words, tone, perception, and comprehension should be neutral for both parties.

4. The personality and behavior of an individual.

There is no definitive answer as to which personalities work best together to create a healthy relationship. This attraction is based on individual preference. In some situations, the appearance, approach, and initial conversation were on point, but the personality and behavior became the first obstacle to the relationship moving forward in a healthy manner.

5. Sexuality and communication through body language.

Communication through body language also shows possible interest. This type of communication is most commonly known as flirting. Flirting can include subtle non-verbal cues of interest or it can include heavy allusions to sexual interest.

1. Prolonged eye gazing

It is considered to be quite intimate to hold one's gaze directly into our own. A long, shared gaze often increases arousal, so a disinterested party might look away. To continue that gaze, acknowledging arousal shows attraction and desire. A mutual acceptance of both will also include a smile or wink.

2. Open body language

Open body language occurs when arms are at the side of the body or rested against something. Arms crossed in front of the chest is a closed body position. In engaging body language and interest the arms are open, leaning forward, as well as facing directly in front of the person who is meant to receive the cue.

3. Lip-licking, biting, or touching

An individual who touches their lips when exchanging a prolonged gaze with someone else is showing interest in the possibility of kissing. Where lip-touching is often a passive, non-verbal cue, lip-biting is more aggressive and shows the individual's invitation for intimacy. Lip-licking is seen as a non-verbal, sexual invitation for physical touch and/or sexual interaction.

4. Finger to lips, breast brush, chest graze

The movement here is hand to mouth. The receiver is watching the hand movement of the other person's lips. The fingers then slowly graze either the breast or the chest. The receiver follows the fingers to the grazing touch. This movement tells them that a sensual invitation has been made.

5. The "accidental" touching

This movement happens casually while two people are already engaged in verbal communications. One moves to where his knees are touching the knees of the other. This could also be a slight movement so that hands graze over the hand, arm, or leg of the individual during the conversation. To show agreement, one person may lay their hand to rest on the prospective partner's hands. This is usually a soft touch with sometimes a slight squeeze of encouragement.

6. The welcoming smile

It is common for people to smile at each other to show happiness or excitement. This smile naturally happens more often between people who are attracted to each other. Coming home from work to a warm welcoming smile can often be an invitation for intimacy or a sexual encounter.

7. Vigorous head nodding in agreement

This type of cue is often subtle to the receiver. However, it is often an effective, positive move to show attraction. Agreement between two people regardless of the topic welcomes a connection through both verbal and non-verbal body language. The sexual attraction, while subtle, builds a foundation of comfort.

8. Prolonged body glances

This sexual non-verbal cue is very bold and can be considered aggressive. To scan the body from head to toes suggest that sexualized thoughts and intentions are already in play. Shared, prolonged body glances, where both parties are involved show immediate connection and interest in sex.

At the start of a healthy relationship, two people will find common ground. This could be as simple as having activities and/or hobbies that both people are interested in. For example, both parties have determined that they enjoy Italian food best. A discussion over dinner will likely bring up work and what they each do to ensure financial security. For a great number of people finding a partner that works in a similar type of job is important. This is because it allows their partner to understand meal planning and scheduling.

This is certainly not for all couples; there are just as many couples that support one another working in entirely different jobs. The factor here is common ground, that is, how comfortable the couple is in discussing their lives. Some couples do not feel comfortable talking about their job to a partner that has little or no experience in that field. At the same time, for some couples, that difference in their jobs is what makes dinner conversations interesting.

While the future cannot be set in stone, it can be planned and implemented with commitment. It is important for couples to share future plans and ideas. Such ideas would include whether or not to have children. Would having children be something that may be considered later in life, or would having children early on prove to be beneficial? Would having children be a deal-breaker for one of the partners? Expanding the family should be discussed early on. A miscommunication or misperception of this can destroy the relationship. When one person does not wish to have children and the other does, the relationship is incompatible from the get-go.

By this point, the couple has grown beyond the initial attraction. They are on their way to a life shared with their partner. With this, the financial foundation for the partnership should be carefully considered and discussed for both the present and future. This includes but is not limited to the couple's living arrangements. Deciding to live together is a difficult decision regardless of whether both partners live alone or with their parents.

Common ground is to the foundation of a long-term relationship. Aimee Hartstein is a relationship therapist. She stated that "the first year is always the hardest, even if you have already lived together." Even for a couple that has decided to be committed to one another, the road can be quite bumpy. The first year is often full of conflict, tears, arguments, apologies, and decisions on whether or not to break up. This is because of the basic differences between people, which are unknowns until they pop up. The statement, "we will cross that bridge when we get there" goes a long way to describe how people deal with their relationship, initially.

Things that make the first year difficult include: differences in manners, self-motivation, experience with cooking, laziness, chores, and how they are split. The couple also has to become comfortable using the bathroom, taking showers, passing gas, nudity, and sex.

Often, people test each other's boundaries by acting and reacting instead of discussing. If one partner feels offended or put off by their partner, it's recommended to express this. Unfortunately, some people don't know how to do this. Reaching this level of communication can be difficult because emotions are involved. "How can I tell my partner I don't like that without hurting their feelings or making myself sound horrible?" or "Should we even be doing this together? I'm not sure how to deal with this situation, but I don't know if this is worth leaving over? I know I have strong feelings, should I stay?" These are normal doubts for couples who are at the beginning of their journey.

We have covered the initial attraction between two people who are first connecting with one another. You should now be able to recognize body language and flirting. Body language is not only used with potential partners, but also friends. Although the intent is different, eye contact, touching to show empathy, and the search for common ground are still there. It's ideal to be aware of how your body communicates with others, as much as what you read from someone else's body language. We have also discussed the success of coming together as a couple. A great number of couples start on the wrong foot when it comes to jealousy and unhealthy attachment. In the next chapter, we will go deeper into where these feelings come from and how to cope with them.

TWO

How to Cope with Jealousy and Unhealthy Attachment

IN THE FIRST CHAPTER, we discussed initial attraction and finding common ground to build a relationship. In this chapter, we discuss a couple who have reached a committed relationship and are now dealing with emotions, such as love and attachment.

Love itself includes many emotions all embedded into one word. Love can be an individual's need to prioritize the wellbeing of another person over their own. Emotions such as caring, worry, attraction, affection, respect, needs, wants, and happiness are all part of love. Healthy attachment includes all these emotions.

Attachment is like an invisible rope that keeps the couple connected. It has variables, which are emotional feelings for one another, as well as the sexual desire to be with another person. Attachment is a connection that creates bonding. Often, attachment increases the need to be as close as possible, both off and online. Emotions create a healthy foundation for a couple in love. Unhealthy attachment, however, causes jealousy.

Jealousy is often a fear brought on by anger or discontent. An example of jealousy is a child that wants the same shoes as the child next door but cannot have them, which makes the child feel resentment.

Where a couple is concerned, jealousy is brought on by losing the attention of a partner. Due to attachment, jealousy is almost expected in a relationship and, to some degree, it can be healthy. However, it is typically very dangerous to the foundation of the relationship. To understand what parts of jealousy are positive and what parts are not, let's see some examples.

Let's take a couple that works separate shifts, Pam and Ken. The only time they spend together is late at night before bed, or early in the morning before one of them goes to work. Ken leaves for work just before Pam returns from her shift. Pam feels jealousy because work gets more of Ken's time then she does. To work through this, Pam and Ken arranged to call each other on lunch breaks to ensure they have the opportunity to speak. This satisfies Pam's jealousy. To deal with her jealousy, Pam should also consider changing her job or asking Ken to consider changing his. Jealousy here is not destructive.

If Pam and Ken were working jobs on the same schedule, the scenario might go in a completely opposite direction. Either Pam, or Ken, or both will begin to tell themselves, "My partner works that shift so they can spend time with someone else instead of me." Then, instead of calling each other at lunch, as agreed, either Pam or Ken might start calling each other repeatedly, interrupting their work. Jealousy is now causing conflict not only at home, but also in the workplace.

It is essential for both parties to recognize jealousy in themselves and each other. Jealous individuals go through mental gymnastics to convince themselves that their beliefs are correct. When the behavior is not accepted as rational, the individual becomes defensive. A similar behavior is displayed when a partner feels that they are treated negatively.

Individuals displaying jealousy might have underlying issues related to trust. Signs to watch include how they feel when their partner is at work, visiting family, speaking on the phone, attending meetings, or doing errands alone. Ask yourself how you feel when your partner is engaging in any of these activities. Does it feel like they might be doing something behind your back? Does it feel like your thoughts and opinions do not matter when making important decisions? These feelings show a lack of trust. Communicate how you feel to your partner. Explain your inability to trust certain behaviors and start working on nurturing your trust.

An example here would be a wife, Tammy, who is aware that her husband, Joe, works with a female partner, Anna, at his workplace. Joe often has team assignments or tasks that he and Anna work on together. It is not unusual for the two to be connected by phone, email, or in person throughout the day. Tammy tells Joe that the time he spends with Anna concerns her. In a healthy relationship, the communication has been opened and Joe should introduce Anna to Tammy. This way, Tammy's feelings can be validated, and she can rest assured that nothing shady is going on between Joe and Anna. It is very possible that Joe and Anna become friends because of all the time they spend together. In that case, the friendship should also include Tammy.

An unhealthy response from Tammy would be accusing Joe of cheating. Tammy may even go as far as to check Joe's messages, read his emails, and call his work to check on how much time he spends there. Tammy would be at risk of losing the relationship if she went this route. Her jealousy is blatantly directed at Anna. Therefore, Tammy may feel threatened and escalate her behavior to a point where it's detrimental both to the relationship and to Joe's work and ability to earn an income.

It's hard to deal with a jealous partner. This could be because they're always apologetic and offer justifications for their actions. You might ask yourself these questions: is my partner not allowing me any space? Are their demands interfering with outside relationships, such as my relationship with my family, friends, or co-workers? Do I feel comfortable spending time with anyone outside of my partner without fear of conflict with my partner? If you can answer "yes" to any of these questions, the relationship is lacking trust.

How do you recognize love and trust versus love and jealousy? This is not a simple question. For each individual, the focus on action and reaction has variables of their own. These variables refer to how and why someone acts in a certain manner. Here are some samples of human behavioral patterns that confuse the foundation of love and trust with love and jealousy. These samples include human behavior as a whole, but also the male versus female perspective, and the expectations of society.

Human behavior as a whole can be explained through the motivation of ownership. While people will say that they don't "own" their partner, the behavior suggests differently. Love has created an attachment to their partner. Love can make people possessive. When acting possessive, people act exactly as if they owned their partner.

Males also perceive love differently from females. While they both act on jealousy with similar results, the reasons for this behavior often differ. Research mostly agrees that women are more influenced by emotion and nurturing than a man. When a woman loves someone, she feels needed, becomes accommodating, and nurtures them. The need to take care of the partner's needs becomes so great that she can feel easily threatened by other people vying for her partner's attention. She may begin asking herself questions such as: "why does my partner spend so much time with that person? Why does he talk to them so often? I am perfectly capable of providing everything that is needed!" This creates jealousy.

A man that feels love for someone becomes protective, feels appreciated and invested in the relationship. His need to be the chief component in his partner's life motivates him to work hard and earn his partner's trust. If his partner is spending a great deal of time with another person, he will question his stability as a substantial partner. He may begin asking questions such as: "am I not man enough, that she needs someone else?" or, "am I doing something wrong, sexually, that would encourage my partner to look for attention elsewhere?" This also creates jealousy.

The way to cope with jealousy is through communication. Communication is, needless to say, key in healthy relating. However, does it ever happen that you think, "I'm talking until I'm blue in the face, and nothing seems to be working." The key to communicating is not just talking, it is how you talk. Earlier, we discussed tone, language, perception and comprehension during the initial attraction. Those key points are just as vital on day one as they are 50 years down the road.

If you are the one that has a partner who is jealous and behaving inappropriately, you may be feeling beaten down and upset because of this. It is now time to work through this issue. Consider having this conversation with yourself before approaching your partner about their jealousy.

- How would I want someone to approach this topic with me, and not upset me? This is how I need to approach my partner.
- What words should I use to convey my point without sounding like I am making accusations? I want my partner to understand the importance of this discussion as a positive move forward.
- How does my partner react to possible conflict? Is this something that we should discuss as well? I want to be as comfortable speaking to my partner about things, as much as I want them to be comfortable talking to me.
- What action has my partner taken that warrants the need for this conversation? I need to explain to my partner that their jealousy and its effect on me are harmful to the relationship.
- Am I willing to accept my partner's reasons for their behavior? My partner's feelings are just as valid as mine.

If you are the one that is feeling jealous and inadequate in your relationship, you know that you are angry and very possibly fearful of losing your partner. In your mind, you are doing what is right to fight for what is yours. Your partner, however, does not share the way you feel. Your actions have brought on a negative reaction from them. It is now time to work through this issue. Consider having this conversation with yourself before approaching your partner about your jealousy.

- What is it that I am doing that is causing my partner to be upset with my behavior? I need to understand why they feel this way.
- How do I keep myself from coming off as defensive, while I listen to my partner's objections to my behavior? My partner and I both need to acknowledge jealousy as a valid emotion.
- How does my partner react to possible conflict? I need to convey my justifications while keeping anger to a minimum.
- Are my justifications for my actions reasonable? Do I have a reason to show mistrust? I need to trust my partner as much as I want them to trust me.
- Am I willing to compromise with my partner's request about my previous behavior? My partner's feelings are just as valid as mine.

Love is not jealousy, just as jealousy is not love. Both are separate emotions that feed off of one another. Taking into account that age and life experiences of people can also be variables in how jealousy develops, it is commonly believed that when two people express love for each other, jealousy is expected. It cannot be said enough that some jealousy is acceptable for a healthy relationship. To cope with jealousy, discuss it with your partner and prepare for feedback. The truth is that this particular topic can be one of the most difficult to openly discuss. That is because jealousy is a strong emotion. Use the conversation starters above and solve the issue. The resolution itself can be a matter of mutual boundaries.

Boundaries are crucial for an individual's well being emotionally, mentally, and physically. It is recommended to have boundaries in a relationship as well. These limits in your relationship are very healthy and beneficial to both parties. You are a couple, however you're also two individual people who need limitations as to what you will allow or not allow. Keep in mind that these limitations are not a dividing line for your couple. To cope with and defeat detrimental jealousy, trust and constraints need to be respected from both sides. When the boundaries feel like confinements, other emotions, such as anxiety and insecurities, can also occur.

In chapter two we covered one of the most difficult topics for a couple. Oftentimes, people do not want to admit that they're jealous because it makes them feel bad. While it is not entirely healthy, jealousy is normal and does not always affect the relationship in a negative way. After reading this chapter, you and your partner will be able to control your jealousy.

Chapter Three deals with anxiety and insecurities. When we hear the word insecure, we often recoil. When someone says, "you are insecure," it's like hearing them say, "you're a train wreck." Chapter three will continue our attempt to understand jealousy while attempting to understand the anxiety and insecurities tied in with it. You most certainly are not a train wreck for feeling the way that you do. Understanding these emotional roller coaster feelings gives you the opportunity to cope with them in a positive manner.

THREE

Overcome Anxiety and Insecurities

IN THE LAST CHAPTER, we talked about healthy boundaries and personal limitations inside a relationship. It is common for couples to misconstrue requests for personal limitations. When one partner appears to be more aggressive or adamant about these boundaries, the other partner may feel anxiety. Anxiety and insecurities work hand and hand to affect a person's emotions and behaviors. We are going to go over what anxiety is and what it feels like. Then we'll cover the topic of insecurities and the behaviors associated with them.

What exactly is anxiety? Anxiety is your body's natural response to stress. It is a feeling of fear or worry about the unknown. The first day of school or the first day on a new job can be an experience that heightens stress and brings about anxiety. A relationship, however, is not the same as working a new job or going to school for the first time. The fear of doing something wrong or pushing your partner's boundaries is a huge source of stress. Anxiety can be born out of fear of pushing your partner's boundaries, or the possibility of your partner pushing your personal boundaries. There are a variety of limitations that a person can have. These include but are not limited to use of smartphones and social media, letters, hobbies, acceptable behaviors, emotions, language, and sex. Here are some reasons that some of these could lead to anxiety.

Smartphones — At this point in time, most people have a phone. The smartphone itself is not just a device to make and receive calls. It is used for a variety of other tasks, including social media, navigation, email, and movie-watching. People can pay for their groceries with their phones. Most people want their partners to respect their privacy by not sharing their smartphones. It is certainly acceptable to share them with a partner, however. Either way, anxiety develops when privacy is not respected.

Social media — With over 100 social media platforms in existence, millions of users are connected globally. Each person has their own personal profile for posting, commenting, teaching, and learning. There are couples that are very comfortable sharing profiles where both have unlimited access. There are also couples that keep their own profile separate. When one partner feels an account should be shared and the other disagrees, anxiety begins to build. One partner may feel excluded. When social media has always been shared, conflict can occur when one partner wants their own account.

Letters — Writing letters to family and friends is personal. Every individual has the right to correspond with whomever they choose. It is paramount to ensure correspondence does not disrespect the relationship. An example here is what I call the "sound board." The sound board is an outsider that offers a listening ear and advice about your relationship. When your sound board gets more attention from you than your partner, you have an issue. When writing to a friend, always make sure that your partner is aware of the correspondence taking place.

Hobbies — It is fantastic when two people come together and share the same hobbies. This allows couples to use their free time together doing what they take pleasure in. This is not always the case, though. Sometimes, one member of the couple likes video games, while the other likes gardening. Giving both time for their hobby is important, and refusing time for one hobby, while indulging in the other can cause anxiety in one or both partners.

Acceptable behaviors — Couples need to meet in the middle when it comes to behaviors both parties find acceptable. When you are the kind of person that likes to live in a clean house, it is not appropriate to leave tons of dishes sitting in the sink, unless you have stated from the beginning that you do not like doing dishes. At this point, you may be asked to vacuum the floors. You and your partner must compromise on splitting up chores to keep a clean house. Otherwise, anxiety ensues when neither party knows what is expected of them.

Emotions — It is vital to know that all emotions are valid. Emotions include but are not limited to happiness, sadness, fear, uncertainty, and anger. With a partner that says things like, "just get over it" or "you should not feel that way," those emotions are turned into anxiety. Don't tell each other emotions shouldn't be felt. Instead, offer support so that the other person feels understood.

Language — Every couple has a way in which they communicate with one another. It is important to understand how your partner takes what you are trying to communicate. How you talk to your partner can trigger anxiety. Particular words, body movements, and tone can cause anxiety. Ask yourself this, "are my tone and actions fitting my words?" When you joke with and tease your partner, do you look relaxed? If not, they may not be able to tell you're joking. They may think you're mocking or attacking them. Take the time to tell one another how you perceived a previous statement. That action can prevent either of you from suffering from feelings of anxiety. Remember that anxiety is often fear of the unknown. Without the understanding of how a statement was perceived, an action receives an unwanted reaction.

Sex — Whereas sex is not the only part of a healthy relationship, it is an important one. A great number of people in general suffer from anxiety because they lack confidence in their physical intimacy. This is the very topic that most people even fear talking about. That fear often leads to awkward moments when trying to be intimate. When people feel awkward during intimacy, they start to feel insecure about themselves. Insecurities are based on an individual's lack of confidence and their self-doubt. Here are some samples of how insecurities are established where sex is the concern:

- A man may feel insecure before engaging in sexual activity because of what may be expected of him. The variables here could be his age and lack of experience, or for an older man, lack of stamina. He may be concerned with his physical appearance such as penis-size and physique. Society's standards may cause him to question his performance abilities. This may be a reason for him to suffer from insecurities. As part of a couple, it is vital for him to express and discuss these insecurities with his partner.

- A woman may feel insecure before engaging in sexual activity because of what may be expected of her, as well. The variables here could be fear of pain with intercourse, experience or lack thereof, and personal self-doubt. She may be concerned with her physical appearance, such as body shape and or height. Society will have her question whether or not to engage in sexual intimacy at all. In a relationship, she will question whether she is able to offer her partner what he wants. She may even suffer from insecurities from her previous experiences or fear that she will be judged. Talking openly about these thoughts and fears to her partner will be beneficial.

As a couple of the many variations, both parties can have equal insecurities. These insecurities are brought on by fear of communication, timing, location, increased drive, decreased drive, or medical complications that can interfere with intimacy. To resolve these is to bring all thoughts, fears, and emotions, out in the open and discuss them with your partner.

Anxiety cannot be fixed by taking a pill. It can be caused by triggers both inside and outside the relationship. These triggers include work expectations, intrusive family members, raising children and even daily activities, like driving. Regardless of the trigger, anxiety which permeates a relationship can cause conflict. This domino effect is also an example of how insecurities occur. Because anxiety can be persistent, it needs an outlet.

Take a look at the list of available outlets below. Whether it is you or your partner who is suffering through anxiety, working together can solve the problem and decrease anxiety. First and foremost, you must acknowledge that you or your partner are suffering through an episode of anxiety. If you're unsure of what is causing your symptoms, seek medical attention immediately.

According to an article from "Good Mental Health For All," these are common symptoms of anxiety:

- Rapid heart rate
- Heavy breathing
- Weakened muscles
- Increased sweating
- Churning stomach, feeling of loose bowels
- Difficulty with concentration or focus
- Dizziness
- Unable to function, frozen in place
- Unable to eat or drink
- Dry mouth
- Tension in neck, arms, and hands

The symptoms of anxiety can mimic other medical conditions. This is why it is important to discuss them with your doctor. Anxiety can be treated with both counseling and medication. Your doctor can point in the right direction.

Outlets to assist with anxiety:

1) Try to learn about yourself. When you have had a panic attack, keep a journal of the incident. Write down what the symptoms were and what was going on around you. Sometimes knowing the exact

trigger can help you overcome anxiety easier and with fewer symptoms.

2) Focus on relaxing. Stop whatever it is that you are currently doing. If you are driving, find a safe place to pull over. Everything else can wait. Nothing is as important as your mental health at this moment. Imagine yourself in a relaxing environment and focus on breathing slowly and intently. Slower breaths will lower your heart rate and provide much needed oxygen to your brain. This will keep you from being confused and disoriented.

3) Take up healthy eating habits. Caffeine and sugar increase feelings of being anxious. Avoid eating candy, drinking sodas, and coffee. Instead, eat fruit and only consume caffeine in moderation. This will avoid panic attacks.

4) Avoid alcohol, or least drink in moderation. Alcohol interferes with the brain's ability to function properly. When you choose to drink, know your limitations and your surroundings. Being hungover can also cause anxiety, which is why you'll want to only drink in moderation, if at all.

5) Use complementary therapies. Therapies that include journal writing, exercise, yoga, or martial arts help keep the mind focused. When the mind is focused, anxiety is less likely to occur.

6) Rely on your faith and or spirituality. Religion can also help you find balance. You don't need to go to church for this. You just need to focus on your beliefs in a quiet place, which also reduces your anxiety.

7) Turn to support groups. With social media being a large platform for communication, a great number of support groups are available for you. Use them to connect to others that have experienced similar situations. Talking about your experiences with others that understand them can make you feel less isolated and alone.

Feelings of insecurity frequently lead to anxiety. Beyond coping with anxiety, you need to understand your insecurities and why they happen. Nobody wants to admit to or acknowledge feelings of insecurity because they falsely believe them to be a weakness or a fault. In truth, insecurities are simply emotions caused by a lack of confidence and self-esteem.

When you feel bad about yourself, you lack self-esteem. Self-esteem and confidence are close in meaning, but not interchangeable. Normally, when one does not have confidence, they also lack self-esteem. To have confidence means that one feels they rely on themselves. An example would be taking on a new task and believing that it will be a success.

Self-esteem is best described as how much you appreciate yourself as a human being. A person that lacks self-esteem does not see their own worth or purpose. They are likely to say things like, "I am ugly, I am not good enough, I am not very smart, and no one can love me." Before anxiety is born out of these insecurities, they can be worked through.

Steps to building up self-esteem and conquering insecurities.

1) Affirm your value. Start with making a list of things that you enjoy doing or being a part of. Go down that list and complete those projects. As the projects come to life, realize that you did them because you have that ability. Take some time to pamper yourself, and when you do this, say these words "I deserve this treat, because I am worth it."

2) Prioritize your needs. While helping others is something you should do, don't do it to the extent where you're exhausted when it comes to your own needs. You need to eat, sleep, work, and have hobbies that fit your own needs and desires. It is okay to put your needs above the wants of others.

3) Embrace the awkward. No human is perfect, and we all have moments that can cause embarrassment. Embrace these moments as a unique part of yourself and allow yourself to laugh at your awkwardness.

4) Challenge your thoughts. If you say something like, "I am not good enough to bake pastries," ask yourself why not. Challenge that statement by purchasing what you need to bake pastries. Do not give

up because the first try is a disappointment. Use it as a guide to what you need to change, then do it again. Imagine yourself baking delicious pastries and think about how much others will enjoy them.

5) Keep good company. Choosing whom to spend time with can be challenging in itself. Family and friends alike can be very cruel and judgmental. At times when you feel that these judgments cause you to question your worth, distance yourself from them. Give your time to those who like and appreciate you the same way that you like and appreciate them.

6) Step Away. Step away from the situation long enough to reflect on your feelings and then come back. Life itself sometimes stings a bit. Accept that the sting is only temporary and that you alone choose your life's direction.

7) Reflect on the good. In school, rather than focusing on an unfavorable math grade, congratulate yourself on the A you got in English. Instead of spending time berating yourself for skills that you do not possess, give extra time to excel in what you love doing.

8) Make time for joy. Find activities that you truly enjoy and fit them into your daily or weekly schedule.

A couple coping with self-esteem may feel like they're continuously driving a car into a brick wall. Whether it is one partner or both, low self-esteem is damaging to the team that you are building together. A healthy foundation cannot be built when battling self-esteem issues. Social psychologist Sandra Murray stated that "relationships are far more likely to be ruined by one partner's self-esteem, then any other reason."

In a study of married couples, Murray found that when both partners have high self-esteem, they will idealize and strengthen the marriage. When a spouse spends a great deal of time always validating the other to increase their self-esteem, they themselves begin to feel underappreciated.

Low esteem in one or both partners has the potential to end the relationship. When this happens, the partner who was suffering from low self-esteem often falls further into depression. The emotions and thoughts that they have become overwhelming. As a couple going through this, there are solutions available. The solutions are not instant and should not be expected to work as such.

Whether a couple has been together for a year or 25 years, changes happen. Events such as moving, loss of family members, changing jobs, or just aging affect us emotionally and mentally. Someone who has never seemed to have low self-esteem before can certainly begin to suffer from it later in the relationship.

Solutions for partners coping with low self-esteem include:

1) Avoid negative criticism, blaming, and shaming. Negative criticism includes the wording you use with your spouse. Take house chores as an example. It is very likely that both parties do the same chore, but in a different way. Instead of criticizing your partner for doing the task differently, ask why they chose that method. Take this time to also explain why you choose your method and then accept each other's differences. Blame should only ever be used when the spouse is truly at fault for something. Remember how important it is to take responsibility for one's own actions. A worst-case scenario happens when one partner is not faithful to the other. A very common excuse for not being faithful is, "if you didn't treat me this bad, I would not need to be unfaithful." This is an often-used rationalization for the cheating party. However, one must realize that shaming a partner is a form of mental abuse that increases low self-esteem. Shaming a partner can also include other put downs, like saying "why can't you act like other people? What's wrong with you?" Do not try to shame your partner into being someone else.

2) Accept the other person for who they are. Do not try to change them. From the beginning of the relationship, it is crucial that you understand who your partner is. Find compromises with your partner so that you can work and thrive together. Know the difference between compromising and changing someone, however. For example, when one partner likes to sleep in on weekends and the other does not, the early riser can start doing tasks to help the late

riser get a head start in the morning. They can also help by making the late riser coffee and breakfast. When couples try to change each other, they would insist that the late riser gets up at the same time as the early riser. This can be even more pernicious. One partner can insist on changing how the other dresses, who they are allowed to be friends with, or where they are allowed to go alone. While the person insisting on these changes may believe that they are doing this to help their partner, they are, instead, making their partner's self-esteem worse and exhibiting unhealthy controlling behavior.

3) Offer genuine praise and appreciation for what you value in each other. Saying nice things to each other seems to become less common as your relationship ages. Not saying things like "you know how much I love your cooking" because you think your partner knows this all too well can make them feel unappreciated. Do not fall into this trap. Thank your partner of fifteen years when he compliments your dress. Offer gratitude for your partner of three years who takes time in the morning to make your lunch. Praise and appreciation need to come from both partners. Think back to when you were trying to seduce or impress your partner. At that time, you routinely thought of creative ways to get them to smile such as, "I love it when you wear your hair like that, it's very sexy." These words should be said decades later as well.

4) Do not become obsessed with perfection in either yourself or your partner. Accept mistakes as a part of being human. As individuals, we often condition ourselves to achieve perfection. Achieving perfection appears to be a requirement in all fields of life. The only person that truly has the right to judge you is you, and you shouldn't be hard on yourself. When you make a mistake, think, "okay, I made a mistake. Let's see what I can learn from it." You should also be able to laugh at yourself when you make a mistake. Think, "oh dear, I can't believe I did that. This is going to be hilarious when I share it with my friends." Whether you are learning from the mistake or laughing it off, do not obsess over it. Apply the same to your partner; they are just as human as you are. That means that they are going to make mistakes as well. It

is always easier to say to someone, "I am only human" than it is to realize that your partner is also only human.

You have just finished going over what anxiety is and how to cope with it. Also, you now have a better understanding of what may be causing your insecurities. It cannot be stressed enough that being insecure is not a bad thing. However, you need to develop your ability to cope with it in a healthy way for the sake of your relationship. For every emotion, thought, action, and reaction that you have as a person, your partner also does. If you work together with this understanding, you can overcome both anxiety and insecurities. Learn to listen to one another. In the next chapter we'll discuss the difference between listening to someone and merely hearing them speak.

FOUR

Listening Versus Hearing

TO SIMPLY HEAR your partner is the easy part. Think about what hearing actually is. It is the ability to hear sounds and movement that create words. Hearing is so much easier than listening to someone because it is an involuntary action and one of the five general senses. No conscious effort is required to process hearing words spoken. One could literally hear the spoken word without having to comprehend or acknowledge what was heard. We can literally choose what we hear and what we do not hear. Selective hearing is an ability that all people have.

Selective hearing happens when you are in a crowded room and are holding a discussion with another person. Having the ability to tune out other sounds and voices to hear only that person is making a choice about what you hear. Another way to describe selective hearing is selecting what is important to hear and what is not. A child who is told by their parents a list of rules automatically tunes out what does not appear to be important. The parent says, "Do not cross the street. I do not want you playing over there alone." The child hears, "Do not play across the street alone" He thinks that playing across the street is acceptable as long as a friend comes along. This is an ability we master early in life and do a lot as adults.

When a couple has a conflict, they hear each other. The louder the conflict, the less actual listening happens. Both parties only care about being heard, and they also are driven by their emotions. Anger increases when hearing replaces listening to each other when a conflict occurs. Here's an example:

Tonya is saying, "Our weekend plans need to be canceled. The water bill has to be paid, and you spent that money on new tires. So, I need to pick up extra shifts at work. Maybe we can do this next weekend?"

Luke hears the words, but his only takeaway is, "Our plans are canceled. Because you bought tires, I have to pick up extra shifts at work."

In this scenario, Luke is likely to go onto the defensive very quickly. Luke did not even hear the last sentence in which Tonya suggested moving their plans to the following weekend. This is because Luke wasn't listening. Tonya stated a fact about their finances and her need to pick up more shifts at work. Because what he thinks he heard was an accusation of spending money for tires instead of household needs, Luke became upset. This whole situation could have been avoided had he actually listened to Tonya, instead of using selective hearing.

Try not to put yourself down if you realize that you have used selective hearing in your relationship. As stated already, this is something that we learn in early childhood. This learned behavior is based on how the brain functions. As children, our brains are still developing, so too much information is difficult to process or focus on. When you tell a child several things at once, they have trouble following and often only hear the last sentence. Adults don't have the same problem; however it is not guaranteed that, just because they are adults, they will not use selective hearing. To truly listen, focus, and retain what is being said takes skill and practice. For a couple building on the foundation of a healthy relationship, it is a good idea to practice listening skills with each other. Not only will this improve basic communication between the two, but it will also make them refrain from fighting.

Listening is not a skill that is achieved quickly. It takes time, patience, and willingness to engage in meaningful conversation. There are tools available to assist with practicing and learning the ability to listen. Here are some steps that will provide you with a stronger foundation for your listening skills. They are provided by Dianne Schilling, author of "10 Steps to Effective listening."

Step 1. Face the speaker and make eye contact.

If you were talking to a child you might say, "look at me when I am speaking to you." This is almost an automatic statement to ensure that you have their attention. The same applies to you. You want to ensure your partner is listening to you and they want to know that you are also listening to them. Eye contact shows both parties that both the topic and the person bringing it up are of importance. In the initial attraction eye contact was discussed as a way of initializing sexual attraction. Listening is similar regardless of the topic discussed.

Step 2. Be attentive, but relaxed.

You don't want to feel rushed or intimidated while speaking. When you are relaxed while listening, you'll likely make the other person more relaxed while talking. Keep in mind how you feel when you are talking to someone else. If they make you feel rushed, do you become confused or agitated? Being rushed can cause you to forget what you wanted to say. When you are rushing someone else, even if it is unintentional, they may also forget what they were trying to say. The goal is for you and your partner to be comfortable with each other. This goes back to the body language used when communicating. Crossing your arms in front of your chest shows a barrier or an automatic defensive move. When the speaker sees you as defensive, they may be discouraged from making their point.

Step 3. Keep an open mind.

Listen without judging. The speaker can read your body language and facial expression. If you make a judgment before they are finished talking, you may miss the point of what is being said. Regardless of what they say to you, they are trusting you with their thoughts and concerns. An open mind and showing consideration to the speaker allows them to be comfortable with you. An open mind also builds trust that they can share anything with you, no matter the topic.

Step 4. Listen to the words and try to picture what the person is saying.

This step is allowing your mind to better process information. Think about your partner telling you about their trip to the mountains for a picnic with a friend. Allow your mind to see the drive, the mountains, and what a picnic on a blanket might look like. Your partner recounts how their friend jumped in alarm when they saw a snake on the blanket. You will be able to envision the scene while also being empathetic to the fear they may have felt. However, it turns out it wasn't a snake, after all, but a toy. As you hear that, you feel relief alongside them. Feeling the speaker's emotions and envisioning their story tells your partner you were listening intently. Intimacy is about physical and emotional connections. Listening and sharing feelings increases intimacy.

Step 5. Do not interrupt and do not impose your solutions.

If you interrupt someone in the middle of a sentence, you tell the speaker that "I am more important than you are," "I do not care what you think," "what I have to say is more important," and "your opinion has no relevance to me." You're basically telling the speaker that they are not worthy of your time. Do not impose your solutions to the situation they tell you about either. If and when they want a solution, they will ask for it. The speaker is looking for a listener, not a fixer, unless they say otherwise. In a relationship, when one partner feels that you're trying to impose your own solutions, they are going to stop talking to you about what matters to them.

Step 6. Wait for the speaker to pause to ask clarifying questions.

Suppose you did not fully comprehend what was just said. When the speaker pauses, go back and say, "Okay, back up a minute. What did you mean when you said that?", and then allow them to explain. When the speaker does not pause, allow them to finish and then ask questions to clarify. Your partner may clarify what is being said without your asking, so make sure that you do not interrupt them. It is likely that you will get more out of what they are saying if you ask for clarifications.

Step 7. Ask questions only to ensure understanding.

It is quite common for a conversation to go astray unintentionally. When this happens, take responsibility and bring the speaker back to the original point. Here is an example. Dayna, your co-worker, begins to tell a story about her Caribbean cruise. She mentions that a mutual friend, Dave, came along on the cruise as well. At this point you jump in with questions about Dave. The discussion continues about his job, his wellbeing since his divorce last year, and how his kids are. An hour has passed, and the story of the cruise has still not been told. What you should have done is ask whether Dave is indeed your mutual friend. When this was acknowledged, you should have allowed Dayna to finish her story. You can ask her about Dave after she finishes her story. If Dayna starts talking about Dave, ask if they both enjoyed the cruise, bringing her to her original point. This shows Dayna that you are actually listening to her story.

Step 8. Try to feel what the speaker is feeling.

Empathy is paramount to developing listening skills. If the speaker is expressing sadness, allow your facial expression to also express sadness. Do the same if the speaker displays anger, excitement, or confusion. Share these emotions with the speaker. When the speaker sees this, they feel that they are connected with you while talking.

Step 9. Give the speaker regular feedback during pauses.

If a conversation starts with, "I saw the house just go up in flames!", encourage the speaker to continue by saying, "That must have been horrible for you!" If you notice that the speaker's emotions do not match what they're saying, nod in understanding. When they pause, you can ask, "How did you feel when you saw the fire?" This will tell the speaker that you are listening and would like to know more details.

. . .

Step 10. Pay attention to the non-verbal cues, the unspoken words.

Say that you begin a conversation with your friend Ahmed, "So hey, how have you been lately?" and the reply is "Oh, I'm fine. I've just been a little busy," followed by a deep sigh. That sigh is an important non-verbal cue that maybe Ahmed is not being entirely truthful. To show that you are truly listening, use that sigh as a cue to engage the conversation. You might say something like, "Wow, that was a heavy sigh. Sure sounds like some weight needs to be lifted there. Do you want to talk about it?" You've already shown Ahmed that you are truly listening. A few other non-verbal cues are much more subtle. These cues are facial expressions of irritation, boredom, or false enthusiasm. Look for signs such as a curved mouth, wide or slitted eyes, slumped shoulders, crossed arms, and hiding tears. When listening, remember that words are only a portion of the message.

How do you feel now about communication with your partner? Do you feel that you are ready to listen instead of just hearing? The purpose of listening is to hear the exact words and ask for clarification. Using assumptions to replace listening is the best way to start conflict. A great listener is not just an ear, they also understand the words and meaning behind them. You owe it to yourself and your partner to truly be a great listener.

Up to this point, we have discussed the importance of communication and how to communicate. Now we can move on to the "what". The old phrase "opposites attract" is very commonly mentioned. One partner is likely to be more outspoken and aggressive in the relationship, while the other may be shier and more passive. In this dynamic, they may have opposing views of personal responsibility in the relationship. The more aggressive partner may want to act as a protector, while the passive partner also feels like a protector, yet defers to the more assertive partner. In the next chapter, we will discuss this dynamic between partners, as well as the difference between ownership and partnership.

FIVE

Ownership Versus Partnership

TO INTRODUCE THIS CHAPTER, we will discuss where this question of ownership versus partnership comes from. In general, people do not feel or think that they own their partner. Most do not even consider themselves controlling in their relationship. Bear in mind that no two couples are the same. The dynamics will differ because of preferences, personalities, wants, needs, and sex. In this chapter we will break down the variables of a partnership. The key in comprehending the variables is to acknowledge your relationship. From there, you can determine whether your relationship is healthy, and you are making yourself and your partner happy.

Do not judge your partner and relationship by comparing yourselves to the couple next door. Their dynamic and preferences may not be the same as yours. You may find some similarities and common ground to build a friendship with your neighbors. That does not mean that your dynamic will mirror theirs. A couple should not compare themselves to others. A couple's relationship is only unhealthy when one or both partners feel unhappy, neglected, abused, or taken advantage of. In this chapter, I will provide a greater understanding of how couples can differ through personal preferences. Along with that, we will discuss ways to ensure that you're building a strong foundation for your relationship. Let's get started.

A. What is a controlling partner?

Psychologist Andrea Bonior wrote, "unhealthy and dangerous patterns are not always obvious" in her article, "20 Signs Your Partner Is Controlling." Controlling behavior is toxic, yet extremely common. It can affect people of all ages, genders, sexual preferences, or social statuses. A relationship can be very healthy to begin with and then turn toxic because of controlling behavior. Bonoir explains how this can happen in a gradual manner.

Prior to sharing Andrea Bonior's list, I want you to be prepared to take notes of these behaviors. Whether it be your partner or you behaving in this manner, there is help available for you. Controlling behaviors should never be accepted or excused. They are detailed below:

1. Isolation from friends and family is a common power move by the controlling partner. This is done by complaining of how much time you spend with others instead of them. They might say, "If you needed me as much as I need you, you would be talking to me instead of always messaging your best friend that I don't even like."

2. Chronic criticism of even the smallest things that is intended to make the partner believe that they cannot think for themselves. A statement might be "I'm just trying to help you because we are a couple. Where would you be without me? You always do the dumbest things."

3. Veiled or overt threats are harmful emotionally and mentally. These types of threats are often verbal in nature. A threat to cut off intimacy, communication, or privileges is a controlling move. One might say "If you don't change the way you dress, I won't be touching you at all. Maybe I'll call my ex and hang out with her instead because she appreciates me." The basis of the threat appears to be minor, as the complaint is about your clothes. The threat leaves you fearing that

you'll lose the relationship, which is completely out of proportion with the complaint.

4. Making acceptance or attraction conditional is a controlling behavior. Saying things like "I loved you so much more when you had a better paying job" or "I thought you were sexy before you got fat" are controlling and humiliating statements. The job or weight change has changed the way that they feel. In order to earn this love back, the partner has to stay within acceptable conditions.

5. An overactive score card of favors is exhausting for the one being controlled. The controlling partner keeps a tally of every small move the other makes. Then they use that tally card to make demands or belittle the partner for not being able to keep up.

6. Skilled manipulators use guilt as a control tool. A girlfriend might say, "I would not be talking to other men if you didn't work so much. You leave me alone too often. What am I supposed to do?" This is a classic move for a cheater to blame fault on their partner, instead of taking responsibility for their actions.

7. Creating a debt that cannot ever be paid back is a bold and upfront control move. The controlling partner lavishes gifts and luxurious meals, as well as expectations of early commitment, and adventurous outings on the other partner. This can create debt, which can trap the other person in the relationship.

8. Controlling behavior also involves spying, snooping, and asking for constant reassurance. This behavior does not respect personal boundaries. The controlling partner can say, "As your boyfriend I have the right to know everything! Why would you keep secrets from me? Are you doing something you shouldn't be doing?" These accusations create guilt in the other party.

9. Excessive jealousy and false accusations are also a form of control. This can manifest as innocuous teasing initially. The person who is controlled may also falsely think that the controlling partner only cares about their wellbeing.

. . .

10. Another controlling behavior is refusing to respect a person's "me time". A partner may ask to spend an hour each evening to write in their journal, saying, "My journal time is for me to be alone and just reflect on my day." A controlling partner might reply, "Well since you need your alone time, why don't you spend Christmas alone as well?"

11. Pushing issues like trust onto someone who is not ready for it is another controlling behavior. Trust takes time. A couple that has been together for a while can trust each other more than they initially did. Accusations of lack of trust or being forced to show your trust are controlling behaviors.

12. Presuming a partner's guilt without cause is manipulation and control. A controlling partner would say, "I saw you talking to the neighbor, you were thinking about sleeping with her, weren't you?"

13. Another control tactic involves starting fights to keep the other party from voicing their opinions. The other party feels that they must relent and apologize just to keep the peace.

14. Belittling or degrading a partner's religion or politics is another form of control. Having different beliefs and discussing them is healthy. It is also normal to disagree with each other's beliefs and debate them. It is not normal, however, to force your beliefs on your partners. Differences of opinion must be respected.

15. Another control tactic involves making a partner feel like they don't measure up to the controlling party's expectation. This controlling behavior starts after trust and commitment has been declared. The controlling partner starts comparing you to their ex-partners. Maybe they cooked better, dressed better, and were more appreciative of your partner. You may start asking yourself, if their ex was so much better, why are they with me? What am I doing wrong?

16. Teasing and putting down a partner is another controlling behavior. A person who says, "Congratulations on choosing the most amazing partner. Without me, you would be nothing!" is trying to control the narrative and discredit your achievements.

. . .

17. Awkward sexual interactions can also be a form of control. Sex is meant to be pleasurable for both parties. When one partner feels inadequate to the other's demands in the bedroom, pleasure and connection does not exist. Sex should be an act that both parties pursue with the same level of interest. If one of the two feels uncomfortable, this should be discussed afterwards. However, when this becomes a common occurrence, something is terribly wrong.

18. Refusing to listen to your partner's opinion or demands is also a power move. By denying your partner their opinion, you're effectively telling them that their opinion holds no value.

19. Pressuring a partner into dangerous or risky behaviors, such as drug use or criminal activity is also a controlling behavior. This tactic is basically an abuse of the other partner's weaknesses.

20. Increasing personal doubt is also a form of control. For instance, Brian is attending law school to become a lawyer. He's worked hard for years towards his goal. Brian's partner says to him, "How can you possibly ever win a case, when you can't take care of yourself? I guess you expect me to be in court to tell you what to do."

B. What is the passive partner and the aggressive partner?

It is a large misconception that the aggressive partner is always the one that is controlling in the relationship. Controlling behaviors occur in all personality types. An aggressive partner is likely to have issues with anger management and coping with their emotions. A passive partner has the ability to use their partner's emotions as a weakness. When a controlling partner targets a weakness, toxic behavior ensues. When an aggressive partner does not have a controlling passive partner, they do have the ability to work together on positive coping mechanisms.

However, aggressive partners can also be controlling. This could be because the passive partner does not want to encourage their anger or rage.

Just like the aggressive partner, the passive partner can be either controlling or not. The need for control is tied into an individual's own personal insecurities. This is why it's so important that couples encourage each other's strength and fight insecurities together.

C. What are the submissive and the dominant roles?

The submissive and dominant roles are not to be confused with toxic, controlling behaviors. For many people who live in this dynamic, the roles also respect boundaries and expectations. Couples on this spectrum have healthy respect for each other and support each other through open communication. There are no rules about who can be dominant and who can be submissive. The roles are not split according to age or gender. They all have their personal rules and expectations. While each couple is different, they do have some things in common. The dynamic does not use control to harm the couple, but instead it uses control for balance and to match each partner's needs.

The dominant partner can often be seen by outsiders as quiet and conservative. Primary decisions for the relationship are made by this partner. They often take on the responsibility to be the provider and protector of the submissive partner. The dominant partner understands that submission is a gift that should be treated with honor. Having the honor of power over another is not to be taken advantage of. To ensure that the submissive partner does not feel taken advantage of, the dominant partner encourages their dreams and goals. The dynamic is activated during sexual pursuits, where the dominant partner is in control.

The submissive partner can often be seen by outsiders as a strong leader and a person that takes charge in their personal life by achieving their goals and reaching out to assist others as well. Most submissive partners require something in their life that allows freedom, which is what they receive from their dominant partner. A dominant partner provides safety and assurance, so that the submissive person is able to feel free. During sex, a submissive partner relieves themselves of any responsibility. Their sexual pleasure derives from not being in control and not having any responsibility.

. . .

D. Boundaries and equality

The best therapy for a couple is the ability to communicate equally in the relationship. Both parties should have equal opportunities, rights, and status. Regardless of what role one partner chooses, such as passive or aggressive, they treat each other fairly across the board. This includes submissive and dominant roles. Equality refers to having the right to pursue any goal that results in self-betterment. This should never be a point of contention.

Boundaries are both individual and expressed within the couple. An example of this is a couple deciding that they will not allow neighbors or phone calls to interrupt their evening meal. Enforcing this boundary is as easy as setting phones to silent and not answering the door during dinner time. Personal boundaries have to do with people's personal needs. For instance, one partner may not have a problem using the bathroom at the same time as their spouse. However, if the other spouse feels this is uncomfortable and inappropriate, their boundary should be respected.

It is important that we bring up the topic of smartphones again. An article on statistics and financial services published in 2018 mentions that "Some 100 million American adults say that they have swapped cash and credit cards for the digital wallets at least once." This shows how important smartphones are to people. Therefore, it is essential to discuss your boundaries regarding smartphones with your partner. Many people in long-term relationships allow each other access to their phones. This is not a hard and fast rule, however. If one partner prefers to keep their phone private, that's their right. Searching through your spouse's phone without their permission shows that you have trust issues.

In this chapter we discussed ownership versus partnership. The most important takeaways have to do with respecting boundaries, trust, and respect. You can also evaluate your role in your relationship. While it is normal that one partner is more dominant than the other, controlling behaviors are not healthy and should be completely avoided. Partners should see each other as equals while taking care of each other.

It is now time to look at honesty, and how it is vital to a healthy relationship. In the next chapter, we will dive into understanding honesty, as well as the harmful consequences of lying. All people lie at some points, but it is crucial that this does not become the core of your relationship.

SIX

The Importance of Honesty

HONESTY IS at the core of a healthy relationship. We're going to start with an example. You're house-hunting. You have compiled a list of requirements that took you a long time to write and put together. With this list, you reach out to a real estate agent to assist you in your search. Your list is clear; you want three bedrooms, two bathrooms, a large kitchen, a two-car garage, and a den. The agent calls within ten minutes and says "I have exactly what you are looking for." You hear that and you expect the agent to be truthful, so you make arrangements to see the house. When you arrive, you see a two-bedroom house, no garage, and no den. The agent insists this is what you asked for. How do you feel? You're likely angry and disappointed to have wasted your time.

Now imagine the same scenario, except it's a potential partner. You have your mental list of what you're after in a person. Your standards may include a certain height or weight, as well as lifestyle requirements, such as not being a smoker or loving the outdoors. Your potential partner seems to meet your standards, so you go on a date. All goes well, so you go on another one. After a few dates, your potential partner invites you to dinner. The place is tiny and doesn't meet their claims of a well-paying job. What's worse, it reeks of cigarettes. There are clothes everywhere. Once again, you've been lied to. You can't build a relationship with someone who misrepresents themselves. Your relationship ended before it even had a chance to start.

People making false claims is unfortunately very common. People believe that lying is an acceptable behavior to achieve one's goals, especially in relationships. There are a great number of reasons why people lie. We'll see the most common reasons for lying below.

In "Verbal Deceit," Robert Feldman, a professor of psychology stated that, "Lying is a very effective social tactic. People do not expect to be lied to; the expectation is that they are hearing the truth from others." Feldman's study and explanations offer insights about white lies, exaggerations, and outright compulsive lying. To understand the importance of truth means that you need to first acknowledge the damage lying can cause. So, why do we lie?

1. To flatter people

Flattery will get you everywhere! Well, at least it's worth a try. Why not offer a bit of flattery to make another person feel good about themselves? After all, it is only a little lie to begin with.

The problem with false flattery is the hurt that it causes when the truth is learned. A person would rather not be flattered at all, than be lied to.

Let's say that you have just had your hair done. The hairdresser did not let you see how it looks from the back. You're headed home from the hair salon. Greta, your neighbor, sees you and can't stop complimenting your hair. You're now feeling very happy with your haircut. Your sister comes over for a visit and can't believe how bad your haircut is at the back. You are now angry at both the hairdresser and at Greta. This is flattery gone wrong!

2. To avoid awkwardness

In an earlier chapter we discussed mistakes that we make as humans. Oftentimes, mistakes are hard to swallow as an individual. Feelings of being awkward come into play. This can make people lie. Imagine a person preparing to park. For whatever reason, this person manages to hit the only pole in the parking lot. Not wanting to admit to their mistake and feeling awkward doing this, they tell a lie. "I think someone hit the car while I was inside the store." This lie does not appear to be harmful in the moment, but in fact it is. The person's spouse has the right to know what actually happened. This can become a source of conflict when the spouse of the person is concerned about what really caused the accident because they care about their spouse.

3. To influence others

Salespeople are really good at lying to influence others. A salesperson will lie about a product to influence a consumer to purchase it. In a couple, one partner might lie to influence the other's decision about something they may not be comfortable with. An example of this would be one partner influencing the other's decision to make a large investment. When this goes wrong and the money is lost, the partner who was wrongly influenced may well feel cheated. They may think, "If they can lie about that, what else do they lie about?" No matter the outcome, both spouses are entitled to knowing the truth. To influence using false claims is a form of manipulation.

4. To avoid a negative outcome

Unfortunately, most people have lied at one time or another to avoid a negative outcome. We learn this skill as young children not wanting mom and dad to know about getting in trouble or receiving a failing grade in school. Children may lie that a teacher does not like them instead of admitting they did not study for the test they failed. As adults, we continue to lie about failure to avoid being thought poorly about. For instance, one partner is terminated from employment. If they were let go because they were struggling to do their job, they are already embarrassed, on top of being upset. To get some sympathy, they tell their partner they were fired because the boss hates them. However, the partner may still learn the truth from other people.

Once that happens, embarrassment will be even worse. This is why truth is always the best policy.

5. To achieve a positive outcome

Lying to achieve a positive outcome is not so bad. After all, the end result is positive. Yet, it is the result of a lie and this can normalize lying in people's minds. An example of a positive outcome from a lie would be convincing a spouse to go for a drive or a walk. One partner might say, "I really need some stuff from the store. Please come with me." The other partner, who may not necessarily want to go for a drive, agrees to help. They end up going on a car ride and having some much-needed time together. The outcome is positive. Because of the lie, both partners are better off. It is difficult to see this lie as a bad thing because of the benefits that it provided. However, a lie is still a lie. The true benefits come from speaking the truth. What the partner should have said was along the lines of, "You've been in the house too long. I think this is why you are not feeling well. I say we take today and make a date out of it." This, on top of being true, also lets the other person know how much their partner cares for them.

6. To make oneself look more impressive

Couples who have been together for a while don't need to impress each other. However, recent couples may try to do so. For example, Jill works as an apprentice, making very low wages. She and her partner, Favesh, decide to invite their neighbors to dinner. They end up talking about work. To impress the neighbors, Jill claims to be a master journeyman, which means she's paid the highest available wage. The situation has the potential to become very awkward. For all Jill knows, Favesh may have already told the neighbors what each of the pair does for work. This means that, instead of impressing the neighbors, Jill has painted both herself and her partner as liars. Now the neighbors will likely not want to continue the friendship.

7. To maintain a previous lie

Lies can evolve into making the person who told a lie into a pathological liar. People who lie for the sake of lying don't have any ulterior motives to do so, unlike those who lie to stay out of trouble, or to avoid hurting someone's feelings. Psychologists do not consider compulsive lying a disorder. However, people who are diagnosed with borderline personality disorder, narcissistic antisocial disorder, or histrionic personality disorder commonly lie compulsively, even when there's no benefit to themselves. They lie because truth is either something they feel is dull, or they prefer to self-aggrandize through lying. An example is saying that you had a great time when you traveled the world in your youth, when, in fact, you only went on one trip abroad before the age of 30. When your parents remind you of the truth, another lie becomes necessary. You tell them that you went on a trip around the world without telling them or anyone else. This is a lie, and you know it. However, you can't bring yourself to tell the truth.

8. To provoke intimidation

Lying to intimidate others is very common. Intimidation is part of bullying and abuse. Intimidation lies are difficult to differentiate from the truth. These lies can evolve from saying, "If you do not change your job, I'm leaving you" to, "I will hurt you if you don't listen to me." These lies can escalate to mental and physical abuse, which is why they are very pernicious. Trying to intimidate anyone, let alone a partner we claim we love, is abusive behavior that we should never engage in.

9. To be vindictive

Vindictive behavior is seeking retaliation for an insult. Lying to be vindictive is a deliberate and calculated act, which is meant to cause harm to another person. Let's look at Matt. He has difficulty letting go of past conflicts and holds grudges for old perceived slights. He and his girlfriend, Emma, have a fight about their finances. They finally make up and apologize about the things they said to each other. Six months later, Matt calls Emma's employer and says, "Emma has been stealing from your company ever since she started working there." This is a lie because she has not been stealing. It is also vindictive on Matt's part because he is aware of the damage that he's doing Emma.

Emma will likely lose her job over Matt's vindictiveness over an incident that she's probably already forgotten about.

10. To seek sympathy

A lie is a lie regardless how big or small it appears to be. This cannot be stressed enough, especially when the basis of the lie is to seek sympathy. Allowing yourself or your partner to lie for sympathy is not fair to either of you. It is always acceptable to be sympathetic and show empathy for your partner. Sympathy builds trust, confidence, and security in your relationship. However, lying to gain sympathy does the opposite of what's intended. For example, Darcy broke his leg. The healing process of this injury took him years because he kept re-injuring his leg. Darcy was in a lot of pain and understandably expected sympathy for his troubles. There is nothing wrong with that. However, Susan, his girlfriend, claims that she cannot wash dishes because she broke a plate once as a child. It is okay for Darcy to sympathize with Susan's fear as a child who broke a plate and was scared of being punished. However, Susan is lying about not being able to do the dishes because of that incident. Her story of the broken plate is likely true, but her inability to ever wash dishes is a lie used to gain sympathy.

Understanding why, when, and how people lie is vital to comprehending ourselves as humans. Most people will say that they hate liars, but refuse to admit to their own lies. In a partnership, we do not want to be lied to and we should never lie to our partner. Honesty and trust cannot be built on lies. Suspicions and doubt cannot flourish when honesty is the basis of the relationship. There are tools you can use when you catch yourself or your partner in a lie, so that you turn the relationship around and stay honest to each other. Here's what you can do:

1. Be consistent. Do the things that you say you are going to do.

Consistency proves reliability. When you say that you're going to take the trash out on Thursday, your partner expects you to do this. By actually completing the task each week, you convince your partner to trust you. In most cases, it's simple things that show that you're dependable. When both partners show consistency in what they claim they are well grounded as a couple with open communication.

2. Do not commit to things that you are unable to do.

If you are not a mechanic, don't tell your partner that you can fix their car. It is appropriate to admit what you can and cannot do. Know who you are and exactly what you are capable of and share that with your partner. Also listen to what your partner can and cannot do. Neither one of you should claim you're able to do things that you cannot.

3. Be ready to hear the truth.

An Arabian proverb states, "He who is a slave to truth, is a free man." One partner may not want to hear the truth when the truth might be hurtful. Nevertheless, the truth is beneficial to both of you. Telling the truth at all times can help you both grow as people. When you tell the truth, you are free from the weight of lying or harming your partner. Relationships are not easy and there will always be issues you'll need to deal with. Telling and listening to the truth will help the relationship overcome all these issues.

4. Avoid name-calling and berating your partner.

Intentionally or not, most people turn to name-calling when they're angry. Anger is not a fair or reasonable rationale for name-calling. Nothing really is. You should stay honest even when you fight. Insulting your partner during a fight does not go away when you apologize, it remains with them forever. Name-calling can lead to low self-esteem, which we covered in an earlier chapter.

5. Do not try to be a mind reader.

Honesty is in part listening to your partner. In spite of the fact that most people feel they already know what is being said, that's not always true. Interjecting a response before your partner finishes speaking is not allowing them their truth. They can't fully express what they're thinking. Instead of trying to read your partner's mind, allow them to speak their mind and make sure that you are truly listening to them.

6. Embrace and admit your mistakes.

Whether trying to avoid awkwardness or negative outcomes, covering up mistakes will hurt both partners. Embrace your imperfection and owe up to your mistakes. Both you and your partner want to feel safe in the relationship, without expecting your mistakes to make you a lesser person. Don't judge your partner's mistakes any more than they do yours. Being a perfectionist may stem from unaddressed issues from your past. Be open about it and discuss this with your partner. Discussing your past may make you feel vulnerable, but it's crucial to building a healthy relationship in which both partners can admit to mistakes without shame or guilt.

In this chapter we covered why and how people lie to each other. It is okay to read this over several times if you are still questioning your or your partner's lies. For every action, there is a reaction, and understanding our motivations helps getting rid of lies. Why we lie is what we need to understand in order to stop the behavior once and for all.

The next topic we will address is respect. Although you are part of a couple, you are still an individual who made the choice to be in a couple. In the next chapter, we will discuss the importance of showing respect to each other, as individuals.

SEVEN

Respect Each Other as Individuals

RESPECT IS an absolute essential asset in a relationship. Respect is something we have even for people we do not know. This sounds weird because, doesn't it? Why would we respect people we don't know? The simple answer is that we are taught to do this as children by our parents. The more complex response is that we tend to show our true colors to family, friends, and lovers. It is an inadvertent thought that "Well they know me, they know who I am." It comes down to a level of comfort which precludes manners, respect, and other concerns. We can show disrespect to the ones close to us and forgive ourselves because we expect them to accept it automatically. This can be dangerous to our relationships. We are not entitled to automatic forgiveness from anyone, and especially not from our partners who we're supposed to cherish the most. To put it bluntly, if you don't want your partner to disrespect you, why is it okay for you to disrespect them?

Psychologist Vladimir Pustovit wrote, "Treat your spouse better than a stranger." You might think, how am I treating my partner worse than a stranger? Make a list of all the places you go to. These include but are not limited to schools, places of business, church, grocery store, laundromats, and any other places you encounter strangers in.

- At the grocery store I gave the cashier a smile. Did I smile at my spouse when they returned home from work?
- At the gas station I said "thank you" to the guy that held the door open for me. Did I say "thank you" to my spouse for the dinner that they cooked?
- At church I said "excuse me" when walking past someone going in the opposite direction in the hallway. Did I say "excuse me" to my spouse when we walked past each other in the hallway of our home?
- At work I cleaned off the tables in the break room so my co-workers can sit and eat comfortably. When was the last time I cleaned off the table at home so my partner could sit and eat?
- Before leaving for work my spouse said "good morning" to me and I grumbled back as a response. When my co-worker greeted me, however, I replied with a friendly "good morning."

If any of these apply to you at any given time in your life, then you are one of millions who treat strangers better than your partner. This is so common, that it confuses us when it's brought up. But we should always "treat others as you want to be treated." The idea here is to imagine every person, including your spouse, as a version of yourself. Then, treat them exactly the way you like to be treated yourself, including when in conflict.

Instead of focusing on how to respect your relationship, let's look at how couples unintentionally disrespect each other. This is because when a relationship seems to be failing, it's very common to blame your partner and not yourself. It takes two to make a relationship, and two to break it. With this idea in mind, let's discuss how to respect our partner by looking at toxic behaviors. These toxic behaviors need to be acknowledged and worked on by both you and your partner. As you read through the list and the information for each sub-title, ask yourself, "Does my partner treat me this way?" Then ask yourself, "Do I treat my partner like this?" Let's go!

18 Signs of a toxic and disrespectful relationship

1. They never put their phone down.

They always have their phone in hand during moments that should be quality time together. Intimate moments take second place to social media. At the dinner table, instead of sharing in discussion about each other's day, they're staring at their phone. Many couples have argued that they never spend time together. That is because they were in the same room together, but focused on the phone instead of each other.

2. Their friends know more about them than you do.

It's not uncommon in a new relationship for you to not know everything about your partner. But you should not be in the same situation as the relationship grows. If your partner's friends know more about them than you do, there's a problem with the relationship.

3. They never introduce you to people that they know.

They seem to always talk about other people. You are never introduced to these people. They may even set up times and dates to spend time with them when you are not around. When you try to mention meeting these other people, you are ignored or brushed off.

4. They only take care of themselves and not the household.

Regardless of how many people live in your household, such as children, your partner doesn't help with chores. They are only concerned with their own problems. When you prepare a meal for both of you, they are not considerate in whether or not you get to eat any of it.

5. They do not acknowledge your accomplishments.

They do not give you any credit for your accomplishments. When you get ahead in your job or finish your degree, you get no recognition. Even worse, they tell you that you only accomplished what you did thanks to them.

. . .

6. They will use every opportunity to make you feel less important than them.

If your partner constantly berates you and calls you names in private, this is already a big deal. When they do it in front of family and friends, this is a deal-breaker. Watch out for your partner saying things like, "Sorry for the mediocre meal. It would have been better if I had cooked it instead of them."

7. They talk about you and to you using derogatory terms.

The "old ball and chain," which people can use to refer to their significant other, takes its meaning from a chain attached to a heavy ball placed on the ankle of a prisoner. So, you can see why your partner would feel insulted when you refer to them that way. Don't use derogatory terms when you talk to your partner or when talking about them. These can be very hurtful to them and the relationship.

8. Nothing is off limits. No boundaries.

Suppose you have expressed to your partner that your medical issues are to remain private. Yet, while friends are visiting, she brings them up in conversation. You shared your phobias with your partner in confidence and they put them on their social media. This is another deal-breaking behavior because you lose confidence and trust in your partner.

9. They hide things from you.

Your partner hides receipts for gifts intended for other people and keeps secrets as to where she is going or who she is spending time with. This can go as far as hiding money for their own use while you struggle with the bills.

10. They make it clear if you were gone tomorrow, it would not make a difference.

Your partner tells you, "You can leave, you only take up my space anyway" or "If you weren't here, I could have my buddy, who I actually like, move in." Say you had enough of such statements and actually leave in a huff one evening. While you're spending the night at your parents' place, your partner does not text or call to make sure that you're safe. This is a clear indicator that they don't care about you.

11. They make other people appear more important in front of you.

Maybe your partner makes you feel uncomfortable if you try to touch them in front of other people. They have no problem, however, with a friend or relative hugging them or holding their hand. When you go out, they leave the table and go talk to other people they know, to whom you're not introduced as you sit alone at the table.

12. They never take your side.

Whenever a conflict with another person occurs, regardless of who it is, your partner always takes the other person's side. They do not ask about or listen to your side of the story. When you come home from work and need to vent about a situation that happened during your day, they ask what you did wrong. They make you second guess yourself because, in their view, you're never right.

13. They use social media to bash you publicly.

Your partner uses their Facebook page or a public forum to verbally slander you. Defamation of your character seems to be their favorite topic. They may join others who bad mouth you. This is a form of public humiliation that signifies the end of the relationship.

14. They criticize your style and appearance.

Your partner may insist that they choose your clothes because you lack style. They will tell you that your hair is not long enough or short enough to suit them. They even act embarrassed to be seen with you in public.

15. They shrug while you struggle.

Let's say you have something that's been troubling you. When you approach your partner for help, they tell you it's not their problem.

Worse, they tell you that you need to figure it out sooner rather than later, "You need to get it together on your own or find somewhere else to go." You are given no support when you struggle the most.

16. They have no concern for what is important to you.

You're telling your partner about your worries about the future, and they appear to be annoyed. Things that matter to you are easily dismissed and your partner acts like you're crazy. You ask your partner to do your laundry because you're running late. You come back home to all your clothes still on the counter, while theirs are in the dryer.

17. They are rude to your family to hurt you.

Your partner might flat out refuse to visit your family. This is okay when there is bad blood between them and one of your family members. However, if your partner does attend family gatherings and displays rudeness, he might be trying to hurt you. If you ask your partner to watch their language around your family and they intentionally do not, they are using your embarrassment in front of your relatives against you.

18. They do not see your relationship as 50/50.

Your partner doesn't take any responsibility for the relationship. Remembering birthdays, anniversaries, paying bills, or taking care of the household do not matter to him. Doing everything on your own is overwhelming and stressful. You cannot and should not take all the responsibility in the relationship on your own.

In this chapter we discussed mutual respect and boundaries. Bear in mind that yours and your partner's boundaries are not the same. Nobody wants to agree with any of the previous statements. The idea that partners would willingly treat each other with such disrespect is devastating.

Often, until we see ourselves and acknowledge our behavior as disrespectful, we do not realize it is happening. Accepting that we sometimes disrespect our partner is a tough pill to swallow. So, in conclusion, don't end a relationship over a disrespectful incident.

Instead, apologize (and mean it) and strive to not allow that behavior to occur again. Work with your partner to always cherish one another and respect your choices and opinions.

In the next chapter, we'll go back to talking about communication, yet in a different setting. Honest communication is extremely important to a healthy sex life, which, in turn, is very important for your relationship and its health. Sex can be a difficult topic for most people. Let's turn taboos into healthy open communication in the next chapter.

EIGHT

How to Communicate on the Topic of Sex

THERE ARE four common types of intimacy that are involved in a relationship. These four common types are emotional, mental, spiritual, and physical intimacy. Relationships can survive successfully if they have at least three out of the four types of intimacy.

Let's start by focusing on these types of intimacy. Each part of intimacy brings the partnerships closer together. The greater the intimacy, the stronger the trust is between partners. People often believe that quality sex is what keeps a relationship going. That's wrong. In reality, a couple that has a great sex life but no emotional, mental, or spiritual intimacy cannot survive for long. Being able to trust your partner with your thoughts and emotions goes well beyond great sex to strengthen your relationship.

The four common types of intimacy are:

A) Emotional — Emotional intimacy is sharing your true feelings with your partner. These feelings include love, fear, anger, sadness, and happiness. Both of you experience these feelings and it is important that you communicate them to each other. A strong emotional connection helps to ease anxiety and insecurities. Neither partner should fear what the other may or may not be doing. The emotional connection allows both parties to nurture your emotions and deal with them within and outside the relationship.

B) Mental — Mental intimacy is like a word game that some couples continuously partake in. Let's take the example of Mike and Jay, who love watching old western movies. Mike often uses a line from his favorite movie to start a conversation with Jay. Jay instantly recognizes the line and responds in kind. Mental intimacy stimulates both partners' minds and may even challenge one another for a bit of play between them. A strong mental connection with your partner helps to cope with the struggles of the outside world. Mental intimacy also gives a couple trust in their mental resilience.

C) Spiritual — Spiritual connections are evident when people refer to their partners as soulmates. Spiritual connections allow a couple to achieve mental and emotional connections very quickly and reach peace and harmony. Spiritual intimacy can be related to a shared religion or spiritual beliefs. For example, for Mandy and John, spiritual intimacy may be worshipping in church together, while for May and Greg it may be acknowledging the equal importance of their beliefs as a Buddhist and a Christian and being able to coexist.

D) Physical — Physical intimacy is about human touch and closeness. This intimacy is achieved through holding hands, kissing, hugging, and sex. All acts of affection fall under the umbrella of physical intimacy. Having physical intimacy in a relationship increases acceptance and connection between partners.

Sex is different for every human being; therefore it can be complicated for a couple to compromise on sexual matters. One partner may like a lot of touching throughout the day, while the other may only like touching in the context of intercourse. This can happen when people are not really a match to each other, or they settle for the relationship because they can't bring themselves to discuss sex. People can openly discuss the other three types of intimacy but have trouble with discussing sex. However, communication about sex is crucial for a fulfilling connection.

· · ·

Ask yourself, what is sex to you in your relationship? Is the act of sex about giving pleasure and receiving pleasure from your partner? Is sex about establishing a physical connection with the person that you love? Or is it a bit of both? Do you just initiate sex and see what happens, or do you discuss your needs and those of your partner first?

Let's start by seeing how you relate to sex and how your partner does. Honesty and self-honesty are extremely important to this type of intimacy for both you and your partner.

*Do I have a high sex drive?

A person's sex drive or libido differs based on many factors. Age and health are two such factors. A couple that has sex quite often also crave it more than a couple who does not. If both partners have a high sex drive, then having sex often is an expression of this. A healthy sex drive does not interfere with daily activities, such as work or social engagements. It's important to understand your own sex drive and how you are coping with it. If you have sex often, yet are not satisfied, the dissatisfaction may stem from other parts of the relationship. If your partner doesn't seem to know what works for you, tell them honestly how and how much you need to be touched and otherwise stimulated to enjoy your high sex drive.

*Do I enjoy sex?

Most people would probably answer "yes" to this question. In truth, however, not everyone enjoys sex. This is something that you need to figure out about yourself. If you ask yourself this question and the answer is "no," you should probe further and understand why you don't enjoy sex. This is also something that needs to be shared with your partner.

*Do my life experiences affect me sexually?

For some people, this question is straightforward because they have not been affected sexually by their life experiences. For others, who have been affected by past experiences, this question can be difficult. If, at some point in your life, you experienced or witnessed sexual assault, this can affect how you feel about intimacy and sex.

*How do I feel when others talk about sex?

When sex is brought up in conversation, you need to evaluate how that makes you feel. Are you comfortable discussing sex or not? Some people can be easily embarrassed at the mention of sex. How you feel about discussing sex also shows how comfortable you are with your own needs and body. Are you embarrassed because society tells you to be? Or does sex just make you uncomfortable? Be honest to yourself.

*Am I willing to experiment sexually?

The question on whether or not you are willing to experiment sexually has to do with whether or not you are comfortable with sex in general. If you fear sex, you'll likely not want to experiment. You should decide what are your hard boundaries when it comes to sex and what you're willing to try once. When and if you are feeling shame about a particular sexual activity, this does not mean that there's anything wrong with you. You need to express and affirm your own boundaries when it comes to sex, just like with all other facets of the relationship.

* Is masturbation healthy while I am in a relationship?

While not all people masturbate, it is reported by medical staff that approximately 95% of males and 89% of females have masturbated at least once in their life. Masturbation is a healthy and safe way to experience sexual gratification. In some cases, masturbation will assist an individual when engaging in sex with a partner, because understanding pleasure firsthand increases the ability to provide pleasure. When thinking about masturbation, also consider how often you engage in it. Masturbation is considered unhealthy when it trumps engaging in sex with your partner or it disrupts daily activities.

*What is it about sex that I like?

A lot of activities are considered sexual in nature. You should feel free to express your particular likes, including fetishes. The only bad sexual fetish is the one that you cannot admit to yourself. Sharing what you like about sex with your partner has the bonus that it will make sexual experiences between you richer and more pleasurable.

*What is it about sex that I do not like?

Same as with likes, you should feel free to express what you don't like about sex. You should also make sure that your partner is fully aware of activities that you don't want to participate in, as well as situations that are likely to make you uncomfortable and trigger negative feelings, like shame and regret.

*What are my expectations of myself?

Knowing yourself and how you feel about sex also include your self-expectations. Are you stressed about how you perform during sex or that you're unable to give pleasure to your partner? Also remember that any incidents that occur during sex are likely the result of awkwardness and should be taken in stride. What do you expect from yourself when engaging in sex? Don't set yourself up for failure by expecting to be a sex god.

*What are my expectations of my partner?

Now that we've talked about your expectations of yourself, let's see what you expect of your partner. Do you expect them to take the lead? Do you plan to take the lead and hope they follow your cues? These are matters that should be discussed openly because neither you, nor your partner can read minds. Not disclosing your expectations to each other can only lead to disappointment.

Up to this point we have discussed how you feel about sex. Having the ability to be open about your own sexuality increases the mental and emotional intimacy in your relationship. We need to also consider your partner. It is common that people get so wrapped in their own thoughts and sexual inadequacies that they don't consider their partner.

* Does my partner have a high sex drive?

When a relationship is new, sex is often one of the couple's favorite pastimes. During the first 6 months of a relationship, it is common that people have sex in the shower, in the kitchen, in the car, or on the stairs on the way to the bedroom. This changes as time passes. This means that you can't judge your partner's sex drive in the beginning of the relationship. As the relationship progresses, you will, however, begin to understand your partner's need for sex. However, the best approach is asking them about it. Discuss how often your partner would like to have sex vs. how often you're interested and reach a compromise if your sex drives don't match.

*Does my partner enjoy sex?

When you're engaging in sex with your partner, pay attention to cues that they're enjoying themselves (or not). If cues leave you uncertain, ask them directly if they're enjoying themselves. Be careful, however, that they may not reply honestly. Sometimes, people engage in sex solely to please their partner. They will even lie about enjoying sex because they otherwise feel guilty or inadequate. Assure your partner that honesty benefits you both.

*What kind of experiences has my partner had that may affect them sexually?

A healthy relationship is about caring for your partner as much as you care for yourself. Conversations about previous relationships and childhood experiences are not easy. To open up a conversation, you should use an example of when you noticed them to be uncomfortable, such as "I noticed during sex that when I tried to change positions with you, that you froze up. I was hoping we could talk about that." This way, your partner will remember the moment and be able to discuss previous experiences. For instance, your partner may have been a victim of abuse or rape. This event can still influence how they behave during sex. Even though they are aroused and quite turned on in the moment, a past memory can surface and ruin their experience. Encourage your partner to tell you about these memories and how they can be avoided during sex.

*How do they feel when others talk about sex?

You may not realize how your partner feels when others talk about sex. At home in the safety of your four walls, they may seem very open and comfortable. It is your job to learn from them about their limitations. They may feel that because they are with the person they trust, sex is no big deal to talk about. In reality, when others refer to sex even in a jokingly manner, they may be uncomfortable.

*Are they willing to experiment with sex?

To learn how experimental your partner is, ask them to write you a fantasy letter. Tell them to be as open as they wish. The idea is to encourage your partner to be forthcoming with their imagination and creativity. Many couples try new things sexually without preparation, in the heat of the moment, and have found doing this very exciting. Others, however, find this approach crude or unthoughtful. Therefore, your best bet is to ask.

*Is my partner's masturbation healthy in our relationship?

Just like masturbation is healthy for you, it is also healthy for your partner. The topic of self-gratification can be very exciting to discuss. The only time your partner's masturbation is a concern is when it interferes with sex as a couple. If you feel neglected by your partner, let them know. It may feel awkward at first, but it is crucial to the health of your relationship. The likelihood is that your partner does not view masturbation as a sexual act, but as a stress reliever that is in no way a replacement for sex with you.

*What do they like about sex?

Use your listening skills here. Having sex as a couple is so much more than just reaching an orgasm. It entails a physical connection between you and your partner. Finding out what your partner likes sexually also strengthens other areas of intimacy.

*What do they not like about sex?

Knowing what your partner does not like about sex has to do with respect. Both you and your partner have sexual taboos and things you find uncomfortable about. It is possible that your partner does not share one of your fetishes. As such, it is important not to demand things that your partner would find unpleasant.

*What are their expectations of me?

Generally, a partner's sexual expectations are related to what you promised them. Be considerate of your partner's expectations by being truthful about your abilities. Don't make promises you can't keep or brag about your prowess. You don't want to disappoint any more than you like being disappointed yourself.

For a younger couple, sex and the conversation leading up to is likely to be a bit awkward. That is because sex is a new physical experience that they are learning as they go. Sex is a very normal physical act and allows us to have a close connection to the person for whom we have strong feelings. Sexual stimulation is accompanied by the release of dopamine. Dopamine gives us the feelings of pleasure, desire, motivation, and stress release. This is why people crave sex. Talking about sex, especially with a partner, should not be accompanied by guilt or shame. It is a natural phenomenon.

The unfortunate truth is that we are ashamed to talk about sex. A great number of people suffer from sexual guilt. A couple that engages in consensual sex, where both people are enjoying the physical, emotional, and mental elements of intimacy, is in a healthy relationship. However, they are likely to be embarrassed or even ashamed if other people are aware of their shared enjoyment. Sex shame and guilt has its roots in the following practices.

*Exploring our bodies as children and being punished for it.

Young children masturbate before they're aware of what masturbation is. They do not know about sex and don't understand what a sexual act is. The child locates their genitals and touches them for pleasure. This is as much a part of growing up as learning how to walk. When a child caught masturbating is punished by being yelled at, hit, or spanked, the child is being taught that exploring their body is bad. When teenagers enter puberty, this drive to pleasure themselves increases. By then, they have learned to only masturbate in private. While privacy is needed in this regard, secrecy should not be needed. There is nothing to be ashamed of about masturbation.

However, many children are shamed for it. Even if they don't remember it consciously, they have absorbed the guilt and shame associated with it.

*Judged by religious ideology of sex.

As a child, I was taught that nobody should have sex before marriage because God was watching and would punish them. Later, I also learned that in some religious sects, couples that were married were not to supposed to enjoy sex. Instead, they would participate in sex solely for the purpose of conceiving children. Birth control is not allowed as the "dirty" act of sex should be blessed with a pregnancy. As an adult, I was introduced to a video titled *The Dirty Old Shoe*. The production of the video was for the purpose of religious teaching for teens and younger women. In the video, a woman had sex with a man while she was in college. They were to be married, but the relationship didn't last. Another young man wanted to marry her and build a future together but knew his marriage wouldn't be blessed because he'd marry a "dirty old shoe." The dirty old shoe is in reference to this woman's body already having been worn and ruined by having sex with another man. This horrible story shows the lasting psychological damage that people from strongly religious backgrounds suffer because of how influenced they are by religion. Sex experts agree that religious ideology is behind a lot of failed sexual relationships.

*Not able to live up to locker room talk.

Locker room talk is not prejudice to any gender. While science explains the general anatomy of the male and female bodies, there are differences that are not generally discussed. The male penis is often judged by its size. Women's desirability is often judged by the size of their breasts. Not all bodies are created equal. Sex therapists suggest seeing our bodies as beautiful and unique. However, that's easier said than done. Even the idea of speaking to a sex therapist suggests that we have a problem. Society enforces the locker room talk by presenting the perfect looks of actors and models, whose perfect bodies further make us feel self-conscious. Men are required to believe that they need a large penis, yet should not have an erection unless permitted, while women are required to believe that she should have a perfect body, yet only take advantage of it to breed.

Couples benefit greatly from getting away from the locker room talk. They need to acknowledge their hang-ups and find the best way to accept their own bodies together.

*Self-esteem issues with our physical appearance.

Both genders suffer from self-esteem issues due to their physical appearance. Body image struggles are intensified by television, books, magazines, and the media. Media does not portray healthy bodies for the sake of health. It shows it as sex appeal; the only way to have that is to have the perfect body. Laurie Meyers conducted a study which found that neither gender actually expects from each other what we think that they do. It is the different treatment of each gender that causes people to have self-esteem issues.

Meyers' findings showed that only 11% of women were concerned about a man's physique. Women generally showed more interest in a man's capabilities to be a good listener, maintain employment, and have empathy. Women agreed that they find height, weight, eye color, and body build sexy. They did not show interest in sex appeal. Around 89% of the women in the study placed physical attractiveness at the bottom of their list. This shows that, if you're a man and you're concerned with your looks, you're worried about the wrong thing. Women are more interested in your mind.

Meyers research findings weren't that different for women. About 35% of the men stated that physical attraction was the most important factor in their expectations from a partner. The other 65% of men in the study placed compassion, respect, and positive attitude much higher their list. The men generally found body shape, weight, and hygiene attractive. Only 10% of the men considered a top model look a major turn on. Approximately 35% of men said that they were physically attracted to women who looked like they cared about themselves

We need to stop accepting the ideals of beauty and handsomeness that are pushed by the media and listen more to our partners. When your husband tells you that you are beautiful, you need to stop thinking he's only after something he may want from you. When your girlfriend compliments you on your new haircut, believe that she really likes how you're looking today. Media, after all, is not part of your relationship.

*Puritans by day and perverts by night society.

To provide an understanding of this statement, we need a description of each word and then an explanation of the statement.

> *Puritans were English protestants of the 16th century that sought*
> *to simplify and purify the church.*
> *A pervert is a person whose sexual behavior is deemed to be*
> *inappropriate, or unacceptable.*

Let's see an example. Meena, who is an artist, holds a session in her studio for a nude painting. Her clients remove their clothes and pose for their portrait. The clients remain unclothed until their likeness is complete on the canvas, sometimes for hours on end. When Meena is finished, the portrait will go into her gallery to be sold. In our society, Meena is the puritan, because she has captured the simplicity and purity of the human body.

Danny is also intrigued by nude bodies. His clients get naked before Danny begins taking pictures. Once the session has ended, Danny has the pictures ready to be sold as part of his portfolio. In our society, he is the pervert because he takes pictures of naked people.

Both Meena and David consider nude bodies beautiful. Why are they perceived so differently? Society has trouble making a distinction between art and pornography. A naked body is nothing to be ashamed of. Sex is not always the goal for which people take off their clothes and pornography is not every instance when a nude body is presented to an audience.

· · ·

*Survivor of sexual abuse or rape.

A person who went through sexual abuse or rape can experience sex guilt. Recovery from rape can be a long and difficult process filled with emotional pain. Survivors who enter relationships carry this baggage with them and their sex lives can suffer because of it. According to the Center for Disease Control and Prevention, (CDC) one in every five people are the victims of sexual assault and rape at some point in their lives.

The guilt or shame that victims have because of the assault exists simply because it happened. Victims of rape say things like:

"I just froze and couldn't do anything." This is called shock and is a normal nerve reaction that the brain sends to the body during an attack. Not being able to move or stop the assault is nothing to be ashamed of.

"I thought he seemed like a good person." A rapist or sex abuser does not have a certain appearance that makes them different from anyone else. For example, a rapist acts in such a way that he will come off as a good person to gain the trust of his victim.

"I had consensual sex with her before." Having consensual sex with an individual at one time does not give them access to your body whenever you feel like it. Once a person does not give consent to an act in the present, it is considered rape.

"I had an orgasm during the rape," Your body reacts to stimulation involuntarily. The body will have the same reaction when going through fight or flight, dread, and arousal. A man that is fighting for his life may have an erection during the altercation because of how the blood flows in his body. When the altercation ends and he is not dead, he can achieve orgasm without direct stimulation of the penis. The same can happen to a woman who is raped; her fight or flight response can result in uncontrolled arousal. The orgasm does not mean that you wanted or enjoyed being raped.

A survivor of sexual assault wants to have a healthy relationship just as much as other people do. Sometimes both partners have gone through sexual assault. Your experience does not have to take over your life and keep you from enjoying mental and physical intimacy with the one you love. Here are some steps you need to take to help yourself or your partner:

*Let your partner know that you love them.

When your partner hears that you were abused, or you hear they were raped, anger is a common reaction. This is part of caring for the other person and showing empathy. This is especially common when the partner was raped or sexually abused while in the relationship. Express your love for your partner. Tell them "I love you" and do it often. Telling a survivor of sexual assault that they are worthy of love can help them get over their shame and guilt faster. Telling your partner, who could not defend you from your rape or sexual assault, that you love them helps them deal with their guilt and shame that they couldn't protect you.

*Allow your partner, and or yourself to open up at their own pace.

Some rape survivors may take a long time before they're able to talk about what happened. If this happened to your partner, tell them you're ready to listen when they're ready. Other people may talk about their assault but cannot tell the full story at once. This is because they are still processing the assault. Listen to what they are able to share and do not press them to go further. Yet other people tell you the story of the rape over and over again. Let them do so, listen to them, and then let them know that they are with you and they are safe.

*Suggest seeking help but take it easy on the pressure.

There are a great number of symptoms a person may have after being victimized in an assault. These symptoms include PTSD and severe depression. Talk to your partner about what they are going through and suggest help, such as counseling that they can get from a rape crisis center. These centers have individual, group, and couples' therapy readily available. However, don't pressure your partner to accept help. Being raped has already made them feel that their control was taken away from them. Being forced into yet another situation that they are not ready for can make them feel raped again, in a different manner. Seeking and receiving outside help happens when your partner is ready to proceed. As a partner, just let them know that it is available.

*Show empathy and caution before and during intimacy.

Talking to your partner about physical intimacy is important for your relationship. Your partner may have difficulty being intimate because they cannot dissociate the perpetrator from you during sex. Show empathy by talking before intimacy. Also use gentle touching, while reminding them who you are and that they are safe. Let them know that they can say "no" at any time. If and when they do shy away or say no, show them that they're in control by stopping whatever it is that you're doing. If and when they decide to try again, encourage them to take the lead. Allowing them to decide when to remove clothes, how far to go, and how to start having sex reminds them that this is a loving encounter between people who respect each other's boundaries.

*Make aftercare a priority.

Aftercare needs to be a priority after sex. Sex is intimate and often makes people feel vulnerable. All that work leading up to sex is quickly forgotten once both people have had their orgasms. A person that has been victimized is often left in an awkward and emotional state of distress after sex. To avoid these feelings, don't leave your partner alone after sex. Allow for some time to cuddle, touch, and talk. Aftercare should be just as sensual as the foreplay before sex. This is often a step that couples do not take time to consider. In reality, it is something that would benefit all couples when they engage in sex. Aftercare should be a part of the sex itself because it shows the strength and comfort level in the relationship.

You just finished reading one of the most complicated parts of building a healthy relationship. Sex can be the number one reason for disagreements, because it is such a private topic. In this chapter, we discussed about both our and our partners' expectations and views about sex. If a couple is able to enjoy sex in a healthy way, intimacy can only grow from there.

In our next and last chapter, we'll talk about building the foundations of love. There are some things to think about and analyze before we start a relationship. We'll also include a checklist that you can use to see if you're ready for a healthy relationship. For those of you already in a relationship, this will be a reminder of all the things that you should do to strengthen the relationship.

NINE

Willingness to Build the Foundation of Love

I COULD NOT TELL you how many times I have heard or seen the words, "I am better off single" from someone, only to learn just a few months later that they're in a relationship. People do want to have love and be loved. The very core of our existence is finding companionship.

The words, "I am better off single" alone are a way of coping with previous heartbreak. Very few people actually enjoy being single for long periods of time. They are either deflecting the idea of a relationship because it's easier than admitting to emotional hurt, or they have unrealistic ideas of what it is to be involved in a relationship. Whether single or in a committed relationship, people often ask themselves, "Am I ready for a relationship?"

There is no simple answer to that question because there are too many factors to consider. To make it easier for you, I compiled a check list for you and your partner to find out where you stand in the relationship. Once you have gone through the list, you will know what aspects of your relationship need more work. You will also be able to recognize what you and your partner have already achieved. As you realize the strength of your relationship, celebrate together.

*Are you ready for a relationship?

This is the primary question everyone asks. Single people ask the question because of uncertainty. A past relationship that ended on a sour note will be emotionally painful regardless of who ended it. Before you ask this question, you should probably try an answer to another question: "Am I ready to have a relationship with someone new?" If the answer is yes, then you can move forward. For most couples, this question may linger for roughly half a year after entering the relationship. This is because during the first year of a new relationship, people are still learning about each other. It can happen that two people come together, but they're not ready to be together. Either one or both partners may come to this realization. Once they do, the fairest thing is to let the other person know. Maybe the relationship is only moving too fast. If that is the case, slow down. You can stay committed as partners, even if you don't live together for a while.

*You have attracted a like-minded partner.

Like-minded, just as we explained in the initial attraction phase, does not mean that you have everything in common with your partner. It means that you and your partner have a common ground and have the ability to commit yourselves to each other and to the relationship. Your differences and similarities will mesh together in harmony, which compliments you both.

*You are self-sufficient.

Knowing that you're self-sufficient is crucial. You have your own dreams, goals, and aspirations. It is important that you realize that you are doing the best that you can, without the expectation of another person making it happen. Let's say you are a writer. Instead of waiting for a partner to come along and encourage you, you just sit down and start writing. Being encouraged and supported is great. However, you need to be able to self-motivate to feel complete.

*You will not settle for conditional love.

Conditional love is exactly what it sounds like. It is love that comes with conditions and/or stipulations. Conditional love is absolutely toxic because it is not love, or what love is meant to be. Being in love is not supposed to be like making a deal with your baby brother.

"Hey, if you tell mom I went to the library, I will clean your room."

This is a common deal for kids who grow up with siblings, but it's not toxic in this circumstance.

If a partner puts conditions on showing and giving love, they are not interested in love. When you know that you won't settle for this kind of love, you are ready for a relationship. On the off chance that you are the partner who conditions giving love, you're also not ready for a relationship. Before you give up on the relationship, seek counseling to understand why you feel like you cannot love your partner with all your heart and no conditions.

*You realize that you are okay.

As discussed in an earlier chapter, peace and acceptance is the final stage in being able to overcome a previous breakup. Without this peace, acceptance, and knowing that you are okay, you risk taking your baggage from your previous relationship to a new relationship. This can hurt both your partner and the relationship itself.

*You do not seek constant distraction.

The need for constant distraction refers to not being able to function alone. In order to be able to function in a relationship with another person, you must be able to do things alone. Simple things such as reading a book, watching shows, going to the movies, and enjoying a game of bowling with friends are examples of functioning alone. It is always nice to share these things with a partner and create memories, but they are not required to validate your existence. Knowing you can do these things alone and feel good about yourself is a sign that you are ready to share your life with a partner.

*You are not waiting to be saved.

Growing up, many people expect others to save them. This is akin to

Rapunzel waiting for her prince savior. However, nobody will swoop in on a white horse to save you. If you're waiting to be saved, you're likely to develop codependency in a relationship. Having the ability to care for yourself independently shows that you are ready for love and a mature relationship.

*You honor your greater self.

Your greater self is the inner you. This is acknowledging your weaknesses and your strengths without shame. Remember that you want your partner to honor and love you. They cannot in fairness be asked to embrace, honor, or love what you do not. Be who you would be in love with, so that your partner can love you as well.

*You have unknowingly thrown out the expectations list.

The expectation list includes things like your ideal mate's look, job, car, brand watch, height, weight, and eye color. The expectation list is akin to creating a spell to not fall in love. The more detailed the list, the least likely it is that anyone can check all the things off the list. The expectation list is very often unrealistic and created to avoid allowing others to get close to you emotionally. When you realize that you're attracted to someone and that list is no longer important, you are ready for a relationship. Love is about the individual and yourself.

*You want a relationship but do not need one.

The idea of a relationship is sharing your life with another individual. The two lives will merge together as they evolve. However, needing a relationship for the sake of a relationship is not healthy. A person doesn't need another person to merely function in life. A relationship is not a crutch for the person's issues.

*You have called off the search.

Calling the search off does not mean that you are no longer interested in finding a potential partner. Those that spend a great deal of time actively searching are the ones that find dealing with an actual relationship more difficult. Active searchers are known as rebounders.

Rebounders have not completed all of the phases of recovery from a breakup. Matt and his brother, Tim, expose rebounders like this: Matt says about his girlfriend, "What do I do? I can't seem to get over her being gone," to which Tim replied, "To get over that one, you simply find another one." This is sound advice.

Rebounding takes things away from the relationship before it can even get started. For those that are single, calling the search off refers to not appearing desperate in gaining attention. For those in a relationship, calling the search off means that the focus is now down to that one person they are with and no one else.

*You smile easily, and a lot.

A key sign to know that you are ready for a relationship is your attitude. A warm smile makes you approachable by others. Whether a relationship happens because of it or not, other people feel comfortable engaging with you. Many times, relationships begin because two people meet through a third party. Kelly just met Dana and was telling him she worked with snakes. This prompted Dana to invite Kelly to a party to meet Simon. Dana said, "Simon, I wanted you to meet my new friend, Kelly. Kelly was telling me about working with snakes, and I know that you love snakes!" Because of Kelly's friendly attitude towards Dana, she met a potential partner.

*You are over the last relationship that you had.

You know that you are over your last relationship and have acceptance. Acceptance is truly comprehending that your relationship is over, without a moment of doubt. This is not easy to do. For example, Dayna broke up with John. She said, "I really like Mike and I want to be with him. But if John calls, I don't know what to do?" This shows that Dayna, despite being the breakup initiator, is still not over John. If she had acceptance, she wouldn't even be thinking about John anymore. There are other signs that you're not over your ex. Examples include checking their social media, calling them for odd reasons, driving past their house, or talking about them to anybody that will listen. Not displaying any of those signs represents your ability to move forward.

*You accept change and are ready to grow.

Accepting change is different for different people. Change comes in the form of a new job, a new home, and sometimes a new relationship. Not being able to change can be emotionally draining. Kyle has asked Lyman to move in with him, but Kyle is often upset and very anxious because Lyman does things in her own way. Kyle believed he was ready for a new relationship but realized that he expected Lyman to behave like his ex. Lyman ended up moving out after only a few months. Had Kyle truly been ready for the relationship, he would have accepted change, namely that Lyman was a different person all together.

*You accept and embrace where you are vulnerable.

There are quite a few things in our life that make us vulnerable. The thing that lets us move forward successfully is embracing those things. Speak out and tell others that the words they use were hurtful. Being vulnerable is admitting to them that their words were hurtful. Take a stand. Cry when you feel the need to do so. Crying is an expression of emotion as both overwhelming happiness and sadness. Accept that you are vulnerable by embracing your need to cry. Embracing your vulnerability turns it into strength. Opening up to your partner requires showing vulnerability but helps both of you grow.

Given that we mentioned vulnerability, I'd like to close this chapter by discussing mental health, which is a topic that many people feel vulnerable about. Mental health is of utmost importance. Being in a relationship means that you need to disclose your mental health and work on making it adjust to the new relationship. You can still have a bright future, kids, a home, and a great job when you have mental issues. However, having a diagnosis can help you make adjustments to your life to allow for these things to happen. Here are some tips for both partners in communicating when mental issues are a part of your relationship.

*Mental health doesn't just affect you.

Mental health affects both people in a relationship. When you have an episode, it also affects your partner. Don't make assumptions about your partner's mental health or about how the other person is affected by your symptoms. Don't assume that your partner knows how to deal with your condition either. If your partner is diagnosed with borderline personality disorder, for example, then both of you have to cope.

*Encourage your partner to get the help that they need.

Help is available in many forms for all mental health issues. Help your partner reach out for help. This includes counseling, group therapy, support groups, medication, and talking with you. Sometimes all you need is talking to your partner and feeling their support.

*Educate yourself.

Educate yourself on the diagnosis itself. Having knowledge of symptoms will assist in preparing how to handle a flare up. There are some diagnoses that include physical symptoms. You can find out if your partner will experience physical disabilities and how soon to expect them. Gaining a deeper understanding of what they are experiencing will also allow you to understand any special needs that you'll need to help them with. There are mental health groups that can help you with the care of your partner.

*Do not get hung up on labels.

Do not allow a label or title of a diagnosis to affect your decision-making. Certain words, like depression, can be scary. However, depression is a condition that your partner has, it is not who they are as a person. Learn the symptoms of depression to find out how you can help your partner when they experience them.

*Pick up some healthy habits together.

Pick up some healthy habits together that prove how determined you are to work through the mental illness as a couple. If your partner has difficulty coping with crowds, go to places where there are fewer people. Plan your shopping trips earlier in the day and avoid large outlet malls that might trigger a panic attack.

*Stick to a familiar routine.

Having a familiar routine every week can help your partner better cope with their mental illness. Have something like a date night, where you connect on a weekly basis to strengthen your mental and emotional connection. Make sure that both your work schedules allow for this.

*Break the typical relationship rules.

There are no exact rules that need to be followed by every couple. There are only expectations as to how a couple should function. Do not allow these social expectations to influence how you take care of one another. For example, Lydia and Meg are a couple who do things differently. Lydia suffers from schizophrenia and one of her triggers is running water. However, she still needed to shower. Therefore, the couple designed their shower stall with glass doors so that they could hear and see each other when Lydia took a shower. This may seem strange, but it worked for the purpose they needed it to.

*Communicate openly.

Make sure that you communicate openly. Discuss the diagnosis itself. Some mental health issues do not have specific triggers. Because of that, they can feel overwhelming. Talk about how an episode starts, what happens during it, and how to move away from it. Tell your partner that they are not alone.

*Take care of yourself.

When your partner has a mental illness, neglecting yourself is common. It is easy to concentrate all your energy on your partner and not think about yourself. However, this is not the right approach. If you ignore your own needs, this will cause you to feel burnt out and even resentful in the long term. Make sure that you allow yourself to take breaks and be able to thrive in the relationship. Ensure that you also get some quality "me" time so that you can continue to care for your partner.

. . .

*Seek out support for yourself.

The same way you should be looking for support for your partner, look for support for yourself. There are support groups for people who care for loved ones affected by mental illness. You can also go to counseling. It helps to speak with people who are in the same situation as you are. You'll feel that you're not alone and this will help you do a better job for both yourself and your partner.

*It is not your job to fix your partner.

Last, but not least, it is not your job to fix your partner. You are there to love, support, and care for them. However, you can't fix them. What you can do is understand their issue and assist with healthy coping mechanisms. Many people think that if they fix their partner's problems, there will no longer be any pain in their lives. This is false. It is simply a belief born out of empathy, love, and compassion. However, it is still false. To see why, think about how you'd feel if the roles were reversed. How would you feel if your partner was trying to fix you? Would you feel broken or unloved? More than likely, yes. You can understand why your partner would not want to "be fixed."

This last chapter covered the important topic of whether we are ready for a relationship. This whole book deals with getting to know yourself. A part of getting to know yourself is being truthful. How do you feel about love? You can probably answer this question in twenty different ways, depending on your experiences with love and relationships. Love does not change, but we do. Concede to love, embrace desire, be conscious of change, and keep moving forward with your partner. As you move away from this chapter, remember that relationships are not love. They are the partnership that we form with the person we love. From the moment we are attracted to someone else, our minds and hearts start on the journey to love. Acknowledging that love is a strong emotion created by a couple's connection allows us to be loved in return.

TEN

Coping with Mental Health and Abuse

IN THE LAST chapter we covered information about mental health and the steps needed to assist one another. It is also essential to cover the topic of mental health and abuse. There are three top scenarios of abuse. The first one is that the abuser has a mental illness and is not fully aware of their abusive behavior. A second one is related to post-traumatic stress disorder that can arise from abuse. Finally, the mentally ill person can be abused by their partner out of frustration or anger.

It is not uncommon for two people that have mental illness to begin a relationship. This is because they have many things in common. Having a partner who understands mental illness and what it does is a foundation from which they can build a relationship. It is up to the couple to make this work. This does not necessarily mean that they will not be abusive to one another but it also does not mean that they will be abusive either. It all depends on the relationship and the individuals involved.

Abuse comes in many forms and is often excused because the abuser has a mental health diagnosis. Being diagnosed with a mental illness is never an acceptable reason to abuse one's spouse. A diagnosis, however, is motivation to understand the mental illness and seek available help.

Below, we will look at a list of abuse and their manifestations:

- **Physical Abuse**

Physical abuse is any action that harms your physical wellbeing. It includes hitting, slapping, punching, or kicking, as well as using weapons to threaten or harm the other person. This form of abuse can also manifest as refusing food or sleep to your partner or forcing them to use drugs or alcohol against their will and then not allowing them to seek and receive adequate medical care for their injuries.

- **Sexual Abuse**

Sexual abuse is any form of forced sexual act that is against a partner's consent. Forms of sexual abuse include rape, forced exposure to pornography, the use of objects in unwanted sexual acts, and the use of sexual commentary to belittle or degrade the partner.

- **Psychological abuse**

Psychological abuse can be even more damaging than physical abuse. Your partner may threaten your family, friends, or pets. They may not allow you to spend time with your loved ones. You may be the victim of gaslighting, where you're accused of flirting or cheating with friends when that is the last thing on your mind. They may also intentionally damage your property or even steal your things. You may start to question if your memory is failing because your partner often says, "That never happened, I don't know what you are talking about."

- **Emotional Abuse**

Emotional abuse occurs together with the other forms of abuse. It includes being emotionally unavailable and dismissive of your worth.

The abuser will lie and cheat, while blaming you for the situation. They may withhold affection and use insults to humiliate and embarrass you and then even laugh and make fun of you because you cry as a result.

- **Financial Abuse**

Financial abuse refers to denying you access to your own money and not allowing you access to your bank account. It can also include having to ask for money above an insignificant amount. Your partner may not give you enough money to cover everyday expenses and humiliate you when you ask for more. They may be monitoring what you're allowed to purchase and refusing to contribute to shared expenses such as food, rent, and utilities. You may find that you're working two jobs, while being chronically out of money.

- **Reproductive Abuse**

Reproduction abuse refers to both coercion and refusal. Coercion is forcing a partner to have a baby unwillingly by intentionally avoiding birth control. A woman may refuse to take a pill and pretend she forgot, while a man may refuse to wear a condom or use condoms that have holes punched into them. Not allowing a woman to abort her fetus is also coercion. Conversely, refusal refers to thwarting your partner's attempts to get pregnant or refusing to get pregnant despite your partner's desire for children, having an abortion without consulting your partner, or forcing your partner to have an abortion.

- **Stalking**

Stalking can occur online or in the real world. It can include unwanted attention on social media and using social media platforms to gather information about what a partner is doing and where they are. It can also include following an ex-partner around in the real world and refusing to leave when discovered. Stalking can get out of control and authorities may need to get involved to stop the behavior.

Regardless of the dynamic in the partnership, abuse is never a good sign. There is help available for relationships that involve abuse, however. If you've been abused, it is not your fault. However, you can get help. The goal is to have a healthy relationship. Sometimes, abuse goes unrecognized, which is why we included these most common forms of abuse above.

Abuse is often tied into mental health issues. Now that we know what abuse looks like, we should identify the mental issues that can foster these behaviors. First and foremost, if you are the abusive partner, you need to acknowledge your behavior. Take responsibility for the behavior and get help. You may be able to save your relationship by coming to terms with what you are putting your partner through. If you are the partner that is being abused, you can also seek help. There are various domestic hotlines that can provide resources. You have the option to leave and work on your recovery or stay in the relationship if your partner is willing to work with you.

There are many mental health conditions that lead to abuse. However, they are never an excuse for abusive behavior. Next, we'll look at some common mental health conditions.

- **Drugs and Alcohol Addiction**

There is a disagreement on whether or not drugs and alcohol addiction is a mental illness. This is because imbibing or taking drugs is a choice, whereas mental illness is not a choice. However, due to the effect of alcohol and drugs on the nervous system, other psychologists argue that addiction is a form of mental illness. These substances change how the brain functions and sends signals throughout the body. Alcohol and drugs alter behavior. You may feel normal when intoxicated but fail to realize how you're treating your partner. On top of causing violent behavior, drugs and alcohol also alter people's memories of events.

- **Aggression**

Anger and aggression typically stem from your childhood. They are difficult to diagnose in young children. They will display signs of anger through hitting, biting, and screaming. This behavior can be steered in another direction with discipline and positive reinforcement. Anger and aggression also appear in teens, because during their development, they are highly sensitive to stress and prone to emotional outbursts. Between the ages of 15 and 18, these behaviors are more likely to be diagnosed as mental illness, which cannot be dissuaded through discipline and positive reinforcement. People who suffer from this illness have trouble in their relationships if they do not learn how to control their anger and aggression.

- **Schizophrenia**

Schizophrenia is a major mental illness. Unmedicated sufferers cannot control or end a particular behavior. Schizophrenia is considered a long-term mental disorder that separates the identity of thought, emotion, and behavior. Withdrawal from reality leads to faulty perception, and inappropriate actions and emotions. The brain cannot isolate the differences between reality, fantasy, and delusion. An individual with this diagnosis has the potential to be dangerous to both themselves and their spouse.

- **Bipolar Disorder**

Bipolar disorder involves strong mood swings between depression and mania. A manic high can last for days or even months. In this mood, the individual will display behaviors of compulsive shopping, will be extremely talkative, lose sleep, and experience an exaggerated sense of wellbeing. For a lot of relationships the manic high is only slightly annoying, but not terribly harmful. The other side of this disorder is depression. Depression can also last for days and months. Depression is more than feeling sad. It includes loss of motivation, fearfulness, irritability, insomnia or over-sleeping, and suicidal thoughts. While sufferers are not normally physically violent, they can commit violent acts. Most often, they tend to isolate themselves.

- **Borderline Personality Disorder**

Borderline personality disorder is very common. More than three million cases are diagnosed every year. This disorder is normally treated with talk therapy, medications, and sometimes hospitalization when symptoms are severe. Sufferers often have difficulty being alone and fear abandonment. Other symptoms include emotional instability, self-image issues, insecurity, and impaired relationship patterns. The illness cannot be cured. If you have borderline personality disorder, you're unlikely to hurt your partner, but likely to hurt yourself, which increases stress levels in the relationship.

- **Depression**

Major depression should not be confused with bipolar disorder. It should never be self-diagnosed. A practitioner's diagnosis is always required. Depression refers to a deep sadness that does not seem to ever get better. Sufferers tend to self-isolate and experience feelings of sadness, worthlessness, fatigue, and anger. They will often focus on negative past experiences. They can become extremely angry over small things that should not affect them emotionally. If your partner suffers from depression, they may not have any interest in spending time with you, going out, or even getting dressed or getting out of bed in the morning. Sometimes, they may blame their misery on you.

- **Paranoia**

Paranoia can be a disorder on its own or a symptom of another mental illness, such as schizophrenia. It is characterized by delusions of persecution, unwarranted jealousy, or exaggerated self-importance. An example of paranoia is thinking that someone is always following you, either online or in real life. Depending on how serious the feelings of paranoia are, they can be very dangerous. If your partner is experiencing paranoia, they can hurt themselves and you. They may even think you're the enemy because you're not sharing their delusion.

• Obsessive Compulsive Disorder (OCD)

OCD does not have a cure. Talk therapy and medical treatment have proven to be helpful to learning to cope with OCD and still live a healthy and successful life, however. OCD's main symptom is the compulsion to give into repetitive behaviors. Symptoms begin gradually and will vary throughout a person's life. It is believed that OCD is triggered by stress. If your partner has OCD, try not to make their symptoms worse by putting them under additional stress in the relationship.

• Sex Addiction

Sex addiction is also known as hypersexuality disorder. This is an excessive preoccupation with sexual matters. Thoughts and behaviors related to sex affect a person's love life, job, and daily activities. The compulsive sexual behavior includes excessive masturbation, watching pornography, cybersex, multiple sex partners, and paying for sex. These behaviors interfere with the person's ability to function, such as going to work when they are focused on the next sexual engagement. The risk here is that the sufferer will force their partner to have sex. Sufferers can also harm themselves and others and expose themselves and partners to sexually transmitted diseases.

• Dissociative Disorder

Dissociative disorder involves experiencing disconnection and lack of continuity between thoughts, memories, surroundings, actions, and identity. People with dissociative disorder escape reality in ways that are involuntary and unhealthy. This can cause problems with functioning in everyday life. Sufferers rarely remember when they dissociate, which can last between a few minutes and a few days. This disorder usually develops after a person suffers severe trauma; dissociation helps to keep the memories of trauma at bay. Trauma can refer to the sudden death of a loved one, a car accident, a robbery, a sexual assault, and childhood abuse. Dissociation can either be amnesia or include separate identities. While initially dissociation helps with eliminating the memory of the trauma, in the long term it becomes a major obstacle to functioning normally.

- **Psychosis**

Psychosis is not actually an illness. Psychosis is a symptom of other mental illnesses, such as schizophrenia. A psychosis episode causes you to lose touch with reality. You see, hear, and believe things that are not real. Because psychosis is a symptom rather than an illness, it can be eliminated when the underlying issue is addressed. Psychosis can cause abuse in the relationship because of the delusions experienced by one of the partners.

- **Post-Traumatic Stress Disorder (PTSD)**

PTSD is a disorder formed from either witnessing or being victim to a terrifying event. PTSD was referred to as shell shock in the past. This is fear or shock caused by a sudden alarming experience. Further studies have shown that shell shock is not just momentary, it can be relived when exposed to a smell, sound, touch, or action that reminds the brain of the original event. This caused the change of the name to PTSD. The most common symptom of PTSD is reliving the trauma. If you or your partner suffer from PTSD, you should seek help to cope both with the trauma and the effects of the trauma.

- **Dementia and Alzheimer's Disease**

There are three important factors about dementia and Alzheimer's disease. They are not a normal part of the aging process. Although most people that are diagnosed are over the age of 65, it is not always the case. Younger people can also suffer from dementia and

Alzheimer disease. Finally, while Alzheimer's disease is a disease of the brain, dementia is not a disease but a symptom of the former

Symptoms of dementia include the inability to think straight, retain memory, and communicate with others. Alzheimer's disease, while very similar, is much more severe. Its symptoms also include disorientation, depression, confusion, behavioral changes, and walking changes. Sufferers often lose the ability to recognize people they know, such as family members or spouses. There is no cure for Alzheimer's disease. However, certain medications and treatments have been made available for the early onset symptoms. The medications have helped increase memory and prevented cognitive decline.

You can find a wealth of information about mental health and abuse. Consider taking the time to do your own research for a better understanding. Most importantly though, do not self-diagnose or diagnose a partner without a proper medical evaluation. .With a proper evaluation and individual treatment plan, your partner can return to functioning normally. As previously stated, support each other, don't try to fix each other. Keep working as a team.

One of the greatest emotions that we are capable of as humans is love. We are some of the few mammals that understand empathy, compassion, and romance. We are certainly not perfect beings. It is okay to not yet fully understand our partners. We can see love for each other differently and it still works, regardless. Don't think that love can only be expressed in a certain way. That is not true. People express love in different ways and that is normal. As we saw earlier in the book, we are all different. Keep in mind that when you enter a relationship, your partner may have a completely different view and understanding of love. Let's look at ten ways we can experience love.

10 Ways to Describe Love

1. Love is security; it's having a partner, a best friend, a loyal lover that cuddles and also acts as a cheerleader when needed.
2. Love is indescribable; it is a feeling that cannot be characterized by words.
3. Love is about give and take; it is the ability to open up and hold nothing back. It's also about listening and offering support whenever it is needed. It is getting involved 100% in the relationship.
4. Love is respect; to have love and give love in return shows a mutual respect for one another as well as the commitment being made together.
5. Love is being in sync; whether it be working and seeing each other in the evenings, or talking on the phone all day long, love means that you never disconnect. Both partners pursue spending time together, whether in quantity or quality.
6. Love is commitment; it is finding the person and being the person that is ready for commitment, which can be terrifying.
7. Love is vulnerability; it is accepting your flaws and imperfections and then sharing them with a partner who can do the same. The hardest thing a human can do is be vulnerable. In a relationship, you are vulnerable together.
8. Love is growing together. There are things in the relationship that you may fight about. Instead of seeing these arguments as obstacles, see them as opportunities for growth.
9. Love is knowing your lover's love language. Know what makes your partner happy and use it. Buy them flowers if you know it makes them happy. Also accept their own love language.
10. Love is healthy communication. Talk about everything, not just through text, but face to face. Say what's on your mind. Trust is knowing that you don't have to hide anything from your partner.

Love comes from understanding what makes your partner happy. It also comes from knowing what makes you happy and being truthful about it. Now that you have reached this point in the book and have touched on every possible aspect of a relationship, you are on your way to true happiness. However, you must persevere. Don't let drawbacks affect how you feel about your partner and your relationship. Always remember what you hold in your heart and never allow doubt to grow.

In closing, we must stress that you and your partner are the most important factors of your relationship. You hold the keys to a happy relationship, whether you are just looking for a mate now or you've been in a relationship for decades. With that in mind, you can start to apply the principles of this book in your own relationship.

Final Words

In the final words, think of this phrase, "They are like two hearts that beat as one." It sounds very romantic indeed! In fact, it is not just a thought in passing or a way to describe a perfect couple. Socrates, the great philosopher who was born in 469 BC started to think about "two hearts that beat as one." Since then, many great minds have tried to explain what that means, including Emilio Ferrer, a psychology professor.

Socrates, who died in 399 BC, was very interested in finding out the perfect definition of love. In the *Encyclopedia of Philosophy*, Socrates stated, "Love is neither beautiful nor good. Love cannot be beautiful because it is the desire to possess what is beautiful. One cannot desire that of which one already possesses."

Throughout history, many philosophers have studied Socrates's words to gain a greater understanding. Some think that Socrates is referring to individuals and their capability to love another person. A person does not feel beautiful because they have the ability to love someone. The beauty that they feel comes from the love they receive from another person. When love is shared between two people, their desire for love is already met, so it is not beautiful or met. Socrates is not saying that this desire is bad either, he is saying that love is just that, love. It's a thing without an absolute description of two people becoming one.

The study of love brings us to Emilio Ferrer's research from 2013. His research thesis was based on the question: "Do two hearts beat as one for lovers?" The study included 32 heterosexual couples that were in romantic relationships. The study also included people who were not in a relationship. Heart rate monitoring was part of the study. The couples sat across from each other without talking or touching. They were only allowed to look at each other. In mere minutes, the women's heart rate matched the heart rate of their male counterparts. Breathing intervals, such as inhaling and exhaling, also changed to match those of the male. To make sure that results were accurate, the women were also tested against men that they didn't know. Their heart rate did not change when tested against strangers. Only couples experienced the heart rate and breathing interval results.

In further studies, results show that people in a loving relationship are healthier. This does not mean that they are never sick. However, it is proven that love offers health benefits, such as lower blood pressure, reduced anxiety, and improved immunity. People that have established a long and healthy relationship tend to live longer as well. Doctor Kirtly Parker Jones researched love and its health benefits. She stated that, "People in loving relationships have fewer doctor visits, shorter hospital stays, less pain, and often have more positive emotions." She further explained this in her article, "Seven Reasons why Loving Relationships Are Good for You." Let us take a look at her studies by breaking down the seven reasons that she has provided.

- **We live longer.**

People engaged in a positive loving relationship live longer. This is because the motivation to be with the partner is great to keep them around. To understand this is to observe how couples behave after they have been together for a long period of time. A couple that has been together for several years and still hold hands while walking together are quite literally living for each other. They have made each other their purpose in life.

- **We heal quicker.**

Dr Benjamin Steinberg, a cardiovascular surgeon stated that, "Our patients with social and loving support recover much quicker." The study shows that people that lack this support have little to no incentive to get better. While the mind and heart are in love, the individual wants to get better as quickly as possible, not just for themselves, but for the loving partner that is pulling for them to recover.

- **We have lower blood pressure.**

It is important to know that even couples who enjoy a great positive relationship can suffer from high blood pressure. You should still see your medical professional for your personal care and treatment, even if you're in a great relationship. However, in the studies, happy couples were found to have lower blood pressure because they were more likely to be concerned with their health. This is an unconscious decision based on wanting to be with their partner for as long as possible.

- **We bolster our immune system.**

Heightened stress from work, school, or family conflicts can most certainly lead to getting sick because our immune system is affected. This happens because of the way that our mind and physical body work together. High stress is extremely dangerous for our health. The body is jilted, uncomfortable, and without defense, which in turn leads to illness. In a healthy loving relationship everyday stressors are much lower, allowing the mind and body to work in sync and better fight against illness.

- **We are more physically fit.**

In a loving relationship, we are more physically fit because we care about ourselves and our partner. Our partner is our best friend and, as such, our greatest motivator. Mentally, we provide support for each other with words like, "babe, I want you to be fit and healthy." Having that mental support is like a physical boost that occurs every day and helps us keep going in a positive and healthy manner.

- **We enjoy good heart health.**

When we're in love, our brain releases helpful hormones, like dopamine. These hormones cause our bodies to feel better and our hearts to remain healthy. We like the feeling of being loved and aroused by our partner. When we take notice of that love, our heart can feel like it has skipped a beat. In reality, not only has it not skipped a beat, but it's enjoying better health than if we were single.

- **We feel less pain.**

Dr Kirtly Jones talked about how we feel less pain when we are in love. She addressed the fact that it is not that we do not feel the pain, but our tolerance of it increases when we are in love. She further explained this by using references from movies, where heroes always save their loved one, regardless of how much pain they have to endure. When a villain causes pain to a hero's love interest, the hero will not hesitate to put themselves in great danger and likelihood of pain to save their partner. Love can definitely increase pain tolerance and allow us to experience feats of courage.

Epilogue

AS WE BRING this book to a close, I want to give you one last piece of advice. This is going to be beneficial to both of you and your partner.

Do not allow negative influences to determine the level of happiness in your relationship. A negative influence is anyone that has an opinion that is harmful to your partnership. People on the outside, such as family, friends, and others have their own agenda. Families often have their own ideas of what is the best for you and will sometimes try to manipulate either you, or the situation. Friends feel protective of each other and have the potential to unintentionally cross boundaries. A friend can put doubt in your partner's mind by making an innocuous observation that can make your partner have doubts about the two of you.

Regardless of the topic, your relationship is between you and your partner. Don't let anyone else intervene between you, neither friends, nor co-workers. Unfortunately there will also be people in your life that try to affect your relationship just to see if they can cause a breakup. In some cases it is because they might want a chance to steal your partner. In other cases, it is because misery loves company. And that is company that you don't need.

Manipulation includes treating your partner with disrespect and telling untruths, so that you question the trust that you have in your partner. Despite your best intentions, friends may decide to introduce you to someone new in hopes that you'll be with someone they deem "better" than your partner. Similarly, co-workers may want to offer you friendly advice when you are having a bad day. However, they only see one side of your relationship.

When you're having relationship trouble, to be fair to your partner and yourself, you need a mediator that understands both sides. This person can help heal whatever ills have started to show in your relationship. But, in the end, the answers are in your and your partner's hearts and minds. Remember, you chose each other. There is a reason for that. Your love is still there.

I'll leave you with this message: love is an emotion that brings two hearts together as one. We all want to have a happy and healthy relationship. To achieve that, listen to each other and take time to remember what drew you together to begin with. Love can only exist when both partners work together. If ever you feel like throwing in the towel, grab this book again. Get your partner and go through it together. As you read through, discuss all the milestones you've passed. As you continue reading, you'll fall in love all over again and gain that happy feeling you thought you had lost.

References

Intentions inspired; Why I chose to be Vulnerable, Gia George 2019

Tango blogs; Am I ready for a relationship. Community Bloggers 2020

Kimberly Atwood Counseling; After care, an important though often overlooked step. Kimberly Atwood, May 12, 2020

The doe; Having an orgasm during rape. " believed the myth and sought violent sex" Journalist Marla, July 2020

CT Counseling; Girls feeling pressure to be sexy, famous, and perfect. Laurie Meyers, April 5, 2016

Healthline; How to overcome your insecurities. Janet Brito. November 21, 2019

Stronger Marriages; Adjust these sexpectations for a better life. Kristen Mark, December 3, 2014

Medical News Today; Why is my sex drive so high. Janet Brito, August 12, 2020

Center for Family Change; Establishing respect for your spouse. Blogging staff, February 6, 2019

The School of Life; The problem of sexual shame. Article bloggers, 2019

Science Alert; What happens to your brain when you orgasm. Sophia Mitrokostas, January 26, 2019

Shakespeare Quotes; To thine own self be true. Nicholas Clairmont, June 6, 2013

FBI History; Bonnie and Clyde. FBI Agents.

Psychology today; Get to know yourself. Meg Selig. March 9, 2016

Psychology today; Unhealthy and dangerous patterns are not always obvious. Bloggers, June 1, 2015

UC David EDU. Emilio Ferrer, Two hearts beat as one.

Wild flower sex; Tips on supporting a partner with mental health issues. Bloggers

Medline Plus; Mental Disorders also called Mental Illness. American Psychiatric Association. September 14, 2014

Health care Health feed; Seven reasons why loving relationships are good for you. Office of Public Affairs. February 14, 2007

CPSIA information can be obtained
at www.ICGtesting.com
Printed in the USA
BVHW040032050621
608823BV00013B/3595

9 781802 936728